Positive Mind Power

(Lessons that Guide and Inspire)

Published by :
Lotus Press Publishers & Distributors

Positive Mind Power

(Lessons that Guide and Inspire)

A.K. Kamath

Lotus Press

4735/22, Prakash Deep Building
Ansari Road, Darya Ganj,
New Delhi - 110002

Lotus Press : Publishers & Distributors
Unit No. 220, 2nd Floor, 4735/22, Prakash Deep Building,
Ansari Road, Darya Ganj, New Delhi- 110002
Ph.: 23280047, 98118-38000
• E-mail : lotuspress1984@gmail.com
www.lotuspress.co.in

Positive Mind Power

ISBN: 978-81-8382-302-9

Printed & Published by : **Lotus Press Publisher & Distributors,** New Delhi-02

PREFACE

The mind plays a pivot role in achieving every kind of success and goal, minor or major goals everyday. Mind Power is something that you work with personally to create a specific outcome that you want. When the mind is focused, directed and working toward a specific goal you begin to tap into the power of the mind.

Once you understand the power of the mind you can begin to develop your mind power. There are specific techniques and methods that you can apply to develop mind power so that you are directing the power of your mind and subconscious mind to help you achieve specific goals.

Mind Power is something you should work with everyday and that means really paying attention to what you think and believe. To work with mind power correctly you should pay attention to your thoughts and beliefs. Your thoughts and beliefs are the real power behind mind power. Because these shape your views on the world and eventually dictate what actions you will take.

Your mind has tremendous powers. If carefully programmed, they can be used to change your life in a positive, healthy way. By following the simple but powerful steps outlined in this book, you can direct the subconscious mind and use mind power quickly and easily.

A. K. Kamath

Other Books on
GENERAL BOOKS

1. Chanakya Neeti **(New)**
1. Helpline for Stressed Parents **(New)**
2. Grow Rich with Peace of Mind **(New)**
3. How to be Fit and Young **(New)**
4. How to Succeed in Life **(New)**
5. 100 Ways to Develop Self Confidence
6. Child Development
7. Abraham Lincoln A Complete Biography
8. Mein Kampf My Struggle
9. Think and Grow Rich
10. The Art of Personality Development
11. Positive Mind Power
12. Travel & Tourism An Industry Facilitator
13. World's Great Authors And Poets
14. Effective Editing Help Yourself in Becoming a Good Editor
15. Smart House-Keeping for Modern Women
16. Develop Super Power Memory
17. World's Great Personalities
18. Personality Plus
19. Power of Positive Thinking
20. Art of Successful Parenting
21. A Handbook of Etiquettes
22. World's Great Scientists
23. Body Language
24. Art of Successful Living
25. Jokes for All
26. Selected Dohas
27. Baby Names for Girls **(New)**
28. Baby Names for Boys **(New)**
29. Art of Public Speaking
30. The World's Greatest Speeches
31. Group Discussions
32. Personality Development
33. Think Positive & Things Will Go Right
34. Once in a Blue Moon (A Tantra Tale)
35. God is Dead
36. Travel India (A Complete Guide for Tourists)
37. Glimpses of Urdu Poetry
38. How to Reduce Tension
39. A Book of Stenography
40. Baby Names for the Boy
41. Baby Names for the Girl
42. Ripples in Tranquil Waters

Lotus PRESS

Unit No. 220, 2nd Floor, 4735/22, Prakash Deep Building,
Ansari Road, Darya Ganj, New Delhi- 110002
Ph.: 23280047, 98118-38000
• E-mail : lotuspress1984@gmail.com, www.lotuspress.co.in

CONTENTS

1

What is Mind Power?

Mind Power is the ability to direct and focus the power of mind to create specific outcomes in life. It is not about being able to make someone else do something they don't want to do. Mind Power is not about controlling another person's mind or imbedding your thoughts, beliefs, memories or images in another person's mind.

Mind Power is something that you work with personally to create a specific outcome that you want. When the mind is focused, directed and working toward a specific goal you begin to tap into the power of the mind. This kind of mind power works in conjunction with the subconscious mind. The mind can directly impact the subconscious mind with thoughts and repeated phrases. This is the real power of the mind. It has the ability to interact with the subconscious mind. Once you understand the power of the mind you can begin to develop your mind power.

You can begin to work with mind power to create specific outcomes that you want in life. There are specific techniques and methods that you can apply to develop mind power so that you are directing the power of your mind, and subconscious mind to help you achieve specific goals.

To work with mind power correctly you should pay attention to your thoughts and beliefs. Your thoughts and beliefs are the real power behind mind power. Mind Power shape your views on the world and eventually dictate what actions you will take. If you believe it's difficult to make money then you will take actions that make it difficult for you to make money. In this example—you're actually applying mind power to create what you don't want—more financial struggle.

Now you can turn things around and being applying mind power to make it easier for you to make money by changing your thoughts and beliefs. Your thoughts and beliefs are picked up by the subconscious mind. The subconscious then goes out and creates the situations that appeal to you that mirror what you believe and think.

The real power of the mind is in the ability to change those thoughts and change those beliefs. When you work with mind power you realize that you are in control of your mind. You have the power to change thoughts that don't help you succeed. You have the power to create new beliefs. Once you plant new thoughts and beliefs in your mind you begin to direct the power of your mind to work with your subconscious so that you enjoy greater success.

Mind Power is something you should work with everyday and that means really paying attention to what you think and believe. Your mind has tremendous power—you just have to learn how to use and direct this power.

To truly develop your mind power and to effectively direct the subconscious mind you have to learn and work with a number of techniques. The best way to do this is to apply a system where you work with different techniques at different times during the day. These techniques and exercises should be focused on directing the subconscious mind. As you work with them regularly you'll develop your mind power and you'll begin to achieve more of what you want.

Doctors and scientists now agree that the mind and subconscious mind shape your life and create your reality. That you are constantly creating your life based on your thoughts and beliefs. The mind's power is infinite and we are simply scratching the surface when it comes to understanding the full potential of the power of the mind.

You are always developing and applying Mind power—you just don't know it. And you are always directing the subconscious mind—again, you just don't know it.

The subconscious mind will create what ever you want—you just have to know how to direct the subconscious mind and how to use mind power so that you get more of what you want and less of what you don't want.

Working with mind power, and directing the subconscious mind is natural and easy. You don't need any subliminal programs to direct the subconscious mind or to develop mind power.

THE CONCEPT OF MIND

The concept of mind is understood in many different ways by many different traditions, ranging from pan-psychism and animism to traditional and organized religious views, as well as secular and materialist philosophies. Most agree that minds are constituted by conscious experience and intelligent thought. Common attributes of mind include perception, reason, imagination, memory, emotion, attention, and a capacity for communication. A rich set of unconscious processes are also included in many modern characterizations of mind.

Theories of mind and its function are numerous. Earliest recorded speculations are from the likes of Zoroaster, the Buddha, Plato, Aristotle, and other ancient Greek, Indian and, later, Islamic and medieval European philosophers. Pre-modern understandings of the mind, such as the neoplatonic "nous" saw it as an aspect of the soul, in the sense of being both divine and immortal, linking human thinking with the unchanging ordering principle of the cosmos itself.

Which attributes make up the mind is much debated. Some psychologists argue that only the "higher" intellectual functions constitute mind, particularly reason and memory. In this view the emotions—love, hate, fear, joy—are more primitive or subjective in nature and should be seen as different from the mind as such. Others argue that various rational and emotional states cannot be so separated, that they are of the same nature and origin, and should therefore be considered all part of what we call the mind.

In popular usage mind is frequently synonymous with thought: the private conversation with ourselves that we carry on "inside our heads." Thus we "make up our minds," "change our minds" or are "of two minds" about something. One of the key attributes of the mind in this sense is that it is a private sphere to which no one but the owner has access. No one else can "know our mind." They can only interpret what we consciously or unconsciously communicate.

MENTAL FACULTIES

Broadly speaking, mental faculties are the various functions of the mind, or things the mind can "do".

Thought is a mental activity which allows human beings to make sense of things in the world, and to represent and interpret them in ways that are significant, or which accord with their needs, attachments, goals, commitments, plans, ends, desires, etc. Thinking involves the symbolic or semantic mediation of ideas or data, as when we form concepts, engage in problem-solving, reasoning and making decisions. Words that refer to similar concepts and processes include deliberation, cognition, ideation, discourse and imagination.

Thinking is sometimes described as a "higher" cognitive function and the analysis of thinking processes is a part of cognitive psychology. It is also deeply connected with our capacity to make and use tools; to understand cause and effect; to recognize patterns of significance; to comprehend and disclose unique contexts of experience or activity; and to respond to the world in a meaningful way.

Memory is the ability to preserve, retain, and subsequently recall, knowledge, information or experience. Although memory has traditionally been a persistent theme in philosophy, the late 19th and early 20th centuries also saw the study of memory emerge as a subject of inquiry within the paradigms of cognitive psychology. In recent decades, it has become one of the pillars of a new branch of science called cognitive neuroscience, a marriage between cognitive psychology and neuroscience.

The subject of memory has also been addressed in highly sophisticated ways in classic works of 20th century literature, notably in the novel of Marcel Proust, and in popular films, e.g. Eternal Sunshine of the Spotless Mind.

Imagination is the activity of generating or evoking novel situations, images, ideas or other qualia in the mind. It is a characteristically subjective activity, rather than a direct or passive experience. The term is technically used in psychology for the process of reviving in the mind percepts of objects formerly given in sense perception. Since this use of the term conflicts with that of ordinary language, some psychologists have preferred to describe this process as "imaging" or "imagery" or to speak of it as "reproductive" as opposed to "productive" or "constructive" imagination. Things that are imagined are said to be seen in the "mind's eye". Among the many practical functions of imagination are the ability to project possible futures (or histories), to "see" things from another's perspective, and to change the way something is perceived, including to make decisions to respond to, or enact, what is imagined.

Consciousness in mammals (this includes humans) is an aspect of the mind generally thought to comprise qualities such as subjectivity, sentience, and the ability to perceive the relationship between oneself and one's environment. It is a subject of much research in philosophy of mind, psychology, neuroscience, and cognitive science. Some philosophers divide consciousness into phenomenal consciousness, which is subjective experience itself, and access consciousness, which refers to the global availability of information to processing systems in the brain. Phenomenal consciousness has many different experienced qualities, often referred to as qualia. Phenomenal consciousness is usually consciousness of something or about something, a property known as intentionality in philosophy of mind.

CONTENT OF THE MIND

Mental contents are those items which are thought of as being "in" the mind, and capable of being formed and manipulated by mental processes and faculties. Examples include thoughts, concepts, memories, emotions, percepts and intentions. Philosophical theories of mental content include internalism, externalism, representationalism and intentionality.

MIND-BRAIN RELATIONSHIP

In mammals, the brain, or encephalon, is the control centre of the central nervous system, responsible for thought. In most mammals, the brain is located in the head, protected by the skull and close to the primary sensory apparatus of vision, hearing, equilibrioception, taste and olfaction. While all vertebrates have a brain, most invertebrates have either a centralized brain or collections of individual ganglia. Primitive animals such as sponges do not have a brain at all. Brains can be extremely complex.

Understanding the relationship between the brain and the mind—mind-body problem is one of the central issues in the history of philosophy—is a challenging problem both philosophically and scientifically. There are three major philosophical schools of thought concerning the answer: dualism, materialism, and idealism. Dualism holds that the mind exists independently of the brain; materialism holds that mental phenomena are identical to neuronal phenomena; and idealism holds that only mental phenomena exist.

The most straightforward scientific evidence that there is a strong relationship between the physical brain matter and the mind is the impact physical alterations to the brain have on the mind, such as with traumatic brain injury and psychoactive drug use. In addition to the philosophical questions, the relationship between mind and brain involves a number of scientific questions, including understanding the relationship between mental activity and brain activity, the exact mechanisms by which drugs influence cognition, and the neural correlates of consciousness.

Through most of history many philosophers found it inconceivable that cognition could be implemented by a physical substance such as brain tissue (that is neurons and synapses). Philosophers such as Patricia Churchland posit that the drug-mind interaction is indicative of an intimate connection between the brain and the mind, not that the two are the same entity. Descartes, who thought extensively about mind-brain relationships, found it possible to explain reflexes and other simple behaviors in mechanistic terms, although he did not believe that complex thought, and language in particular, could be explained by reference to the physical brain alone.

PHILOSOPHY OF MIND

Philosophy of mind is the branch of philosophy that studies the nature of the mind, mental events, mental functions, mental properties, consciousness and their relationship to the physical body. The mind-body problem, i.e. the relationship of the mind to the body, is commonly seen as the central issue in philosophy of mind, although there are other issues concerning the nature of the mind that do not involve its relation to the physical body.

Dualism and monism are the two major schools of thought that attempt to resolve the mind-body problem. Dualism is the position that mind and body are in some way separate from each other. It can be traced back to Plato, Aristotle and the *Samkhya* and Yoga schools of Hindu philosophy, but it was most precisely formulated by René Descartes in the 17th century. Substance dualists argue that the mind is an independently existing substance, whereas Property dualists maintain that the mind is a group of independent properties that emerge from and cannot be reduced to the brain, but that it is not a distinct substance.

The 20th century philosopher Martin Heidegger suggested that subjective experience and activity cannot be made sense of in terms of Cartesian "substances" that bear "properties" at all. This is because the nature of subjective, qualitative experience is incoherent in terms of—or semantically incommensurable with the concept of—substances that bear properties. This is a fundamentally ontological argument.

Mind/Body Perspectives

Monism is the position that mind and body are not physiologically and ontologically distinct kinds of entities. This view was first advocated in Western Philosophy by Parmenides in the 5th century BC and was later espoused by the 17th century rationalist Baruch Spinoza. According to Spinoza's dual-aspect theory, mind and body are two aspects of an underlying reality which he variously described as "Nature" or "God".

Physicalists argue that only the entities postulated by physical theory exist, and that the mind will eventually be explained in terms of these entities as physical theory continues to evolve.

Idealists maintain that the mind is all that exists and that the external world is either mental itself, or an illusion created by the mind.

Neutral monists adhere to the position that perceived things in the world can be regarded as either physical or mental depending on whether one is interested in their relationship to other things in the world or their relationship to the perceiver. For example, a red spot on a wall is physical in its dependence on the wall and the pigment of which it is made, but it is mental in so far as its perceived redness depends on the workings of the visual system. Unlike dual-aspect theory, neutral monism does not posit a more fundamental substance of which mind and body are aspects.

The most common monisms in the 20th and 21st centuries have all been variations of physicalism; these positions include behaviorism, the type identity theory, anomalous monism and functionalism.

Many modern philosophers of mind adopt either a reductive or non-reductive physicalist position, maintaining in their different ways that the mind is not something separate from the body. These approaches have been particularly influential in the sciences, e.g. in the fields of sociobiology, computer science, evolutionary psychology and the various neurosciences. Other philosophers, however, adopt a non-physicalist position which challenges the notion that the mind is a purely physical construct.

Reductive physicalists assert that all mental states and properties will eventually be explained by scientific accounts of physiological processes and states.

Non-reductive physicalists argue that although the brain is all there is to the mind, the predicates and vocabulary used in mental descriptions and explanations are indispensable, and cannot be reduced to the language and lower-level explanations of physical science.

Continued neuroscientific progress has helped to clarify some of these issues. However, they are far from having been resolved, and modern philosophers of mind continue to ask how (if at all) the subjective qualities and the intentionality (aboutness) of mental states and properties can be explained in naturalistic terms.

SCIENCE OF MIND

Psychology is the scientific study of human behaviour, mental functioning, and experience; noology, the study of thought. As both an academic and applied discipline, Psychology involves the scientific study of mental processes such as perception, cognition, emotion, personality, as well as environmental influences, such as social and cultural influences, and interpersonal relationships, in order to devise theories of human behaviour. Psychology also refers to the application of such knowledge to various spheres of human activity, including problems of individuals' daily lives and the treatment of mental health problems.

Psychology differs from the other social sciences due to its focus on experimentation at the scale of the individual, or individuals in small groups as opposed to large groups, institutions or societies. Historically, psychology differed from biology and neuroscience in that it was primarily concerned with mind rather than brain. Modern psychological science incorporates physiological and neurological processes into its conceptions of perception, cognition, behaviour, and mental disorders.

Evolutionary Psychology (EP) is an approach within psychology that examines psychological traits—such as memory, perception, or language—from a Darwinian evolutionary perspective. It seeks to explain how many human psychological traits are evolved adaptations, that is, the functional products of natural selection or sexual selection. Adaptationist thinking about physiological mechanisms, such as the heart, lungs, and immune system, is common in evolutionary biology. Evolutionary psychology applies the same thinking to psychology.

HEALTH OF THE MIND

By analogy with the health of the body, one can speak metaphorically of a state of health of the mind, or mental health. Merriam-Webster defines mental health as "A state of emotional and psychological well-being in which an individual is able to use his or her cognitive and emotional capabilities, function in society, and meet the ordinary demands of everyday life." According to the World Health Organization (WHO), there is no one "official" definition of mental health. Cultural differences, subjective assessments, and competing professional theories all affect how "mental health" is defined. In general, most experts agree that "mental health" and "mental illness" are not opposites. In other words, the absence of a recognized mental disorder is not necessarily an indicator of mental health.

One way to think about mental health is by looking at how effectively and successfully a person functions. Feeling capable and competent; being able to handle normal levels of stress, maintaining satisfying relationships, and leading an independent life; and being able to "bounce back," or recover from difficult situations, are all signs of mental health.

Psychotherapy is an interpersonal, relational intervention used by trained psychotherapists to aid clients in problems of living. This usually includes increasing individual sense of well-being and reducing subjective discomforting experience. Psychotherapists employ a range of techniques based on experiential relationship building, dialogue, communication and behaviour change and that are designed to improve the mental health of a client or patient, or to improve group relationships. Most forms of psychotherapy use only spoken conversation, though some also use various other forms of communication such as the written word, art, drama, narrative story, or therapeutic touch. Psychotherapy occurs within a structured encounter between a trained therapist and client(s). Purposeful, theoretically based psychotherapy began in the 19th century with psychoanalysis; since then, scores of other approaches have been developed and continue to be created.

POWER OF THE MIND

Our mind is immensely powerful. Just like a magnet attracts some and repels some objects, our minds too have similar characteristic. You can confirm this by examining the people around you. They pass through some common and some dissimilar circumstances and events. Some of these events or tasks can be completed by some of them easily and some find it extremely tough to accomplish those tasks.

Our mind is nothing but a generator of thoughts. These thoughts become magnets and send out magnetic currents. Any action or idea will be perceived by you as you see and think about it. The more optimistic you are, the event becomes good for you. On the contrary if you develop a negative attitude, you are sure to attract negative things into your life.

The more you think about a certain issue, the higher are the chances that they will get attracted into your life. Having said that, it does not mean that all you think will become real. Thoughts need a particular strength to materialize. Weak magnets do not attract much, and so do weak thoughts.

All of us aware about the fact the magnet can attract metals. The stronger and bigger the magnet, the bigger objects get attracted. Another characteristic typical of magnets is that while one side attracts, it can repel objects too. Attraction, is an unbiased or neutral power. The magnet attracts everything that is iron, irrespective of whether it is useful or not. Same is the case with our mind and thoughts. Be positive and optimistic if you want good things happen in you life, and if you act otherwise you are sure to end up with a lot of negative things in your life. Our brains are like magnets. If they can attract, they can repel too. Any negative thoughts like incompetence, fear, inferiority complex, self-doubt will drive a lot of good things away from your life. These thoughts will be the very factors and will act as a wind that would carry good things away from your life.

You can definitely train you brain to have positive energy. Concentration, passion and belief are some of the tools you can use and apply to charge up your brain with positive thoughts and energy. For many, powering up mind becomes a constant activity. They are not even aware that their minds are charging up. It becomes so much part of their daily routine. You just have to know the correct method and you too can empower your brain so as to change your life in a positive way.

There are many techniques you can try out to empower your mind. Visualization, passion, repeating thoughts, focusing on thoughts are some. Whatever you think, they get transmitted and may match waves transmitted by other people. This may lead to collaboration between you and people who have thoughts similar to yours. You will find numerous opportunities that come up your way. You will find such experiences very positive and will boost your confidence a lot.

Isn't it prudent to channel your thoughts to be positive and beneficial to you? This will make positive things get attracted into your life. Your mind has a lot of untapped magnetic power which you can utilize to attract positive people, circumstances and opportunities into your life. The basic rule is pretty simple. Whatever you think about with great desire and focus will invariably get attracted to you. It may something spiritual or materialistic, but it will come into your life. The power of attraction is omnipresent and applicable to all. It is one of the prime sources due to which our world exists today.

How to Understand Power of Mind for Everyone

Back in the 1980s there was a commercial, a slogan really,

"The mind is a terrible thing to waste". While the commercial dealt with teens and drug use, the message can still be applied today. The power of mind is also a power you can harness to create the life you want.

You're certainly at least somewhat familiar with The Secret, whether or not you've ever read the book or watched the film, you probably know the basics of the law of attraction which is the central idea of the work.

The idea behind this is to let everyone know you can create events in your life simply by thinking about them subconsciously. Since there is a positive and negative side to this, you just need to train your subconscious to believe in the positive.

One prime example of mind power at work is called the placebo effect. This is named for the clinical trials which use placebos for the control group while giving the actual medication to the other. Both groups think they're getting the medication, so both often believe them to be experiencing the effects that have been described to them.

You must have seen people who imagine themselves to be sick and then actually experience it. Similarly people can imagine themselves well and miraculously recover.

We can have a hand on example of this principle. Someday in the morning when we awoke from the sleep and in our mind we are in fact thinking that the day may not go well or it will boring, the day really turns out to be one of those when nothing good would happen. It has to do with the power of your mind—when you think a day is going to be a bad then your subconscious has the ability to make this happen.

There has actually been a lot of hard scientific evidence to back this up. Quantum mechanics explains that at the subatomic level there is no such thing as matter; it is just energy. Experiments have shown that incredibly this 'energy' only exists because it is being observed. That means that it only exists because of the mind of the observer; this the real power of the mind!

There are scientists who are of the opinion that some of the things generally regarded as being supernatural phenomena such as extrasensory perception, remote viewing and astral projection may be explainable through science, although the way that they work is not yet entirely understood. On the extreme end, this leads to solipsism, the belief that nothing is real until you observe it, and the question of 'If a tree falls in the woods, and nobody's around, does it make any sound?'

There are perhaps a very small amount of people who have really thought about using the power of the mind in order to achieve something good and make our lives better from the way they are. It is in fact a prudent thing if we really have our minds working and try and use its power to live a better life. Moreover assets are always meant to be used in a good way before they start being used in the other way round. So where does it all start? How about figuring out where you want to go.

One important thing to keep in mind is that it is far easier to focus your mind to achieve a specific goal rather than a general one.

Pull yourself away from distracting influences. Keep that effort constant. Try to clear your mind of the usual pattern of thirty different thoughts running at once.

There are some people who have a great knowledge of their own mind power and hence work in improving it at all times. This is further developed when they are able to completely channelize their thoughts to the goal they desire to achieve.

This means that the full power of the mind is focused on the goal. With the mind being the ruling power, and these people making sure that all of their other forces are directed at goal attainment, the goal becomes a reality.

Imagine completely altering your life by actively taking part in the influence your mind has on your reality. Say that you wanted a new house. You want that new house so much that it almost becomes an obsession. You think about it all the time, you have even planned the landscape and the colour of the master bathroom.

Ensure that everything you do is focused towards getting that dream home. You may have to work a bit harder at work for example. You could even check out the rest mortgage rates even if you can't afford it at the moment. You can even buy a few things to put into your new home.

By focusing on this goal and putting your mental energy towards your objective, you can make it happen—don't be too surprised when your dream home goes on the market and your offer is accepted; and you even get just the right mortgage. It is the power of the mind which has made this come about, not simply good luck. This is something you can do; something everyone can do. Believe in the power of your mind and you can achieve anything—set your mind on a small goal and work your way up to bigger and better things as you go.

'Mind over Matter'

Power of the human mind as expressed correctly in the idiom 'mind over matter' is immense and vast. This is undoubtedly true since starting from concentration to willpower that is used for self-development, from bearing pain by focusing your mind elsewhere to even moving matter with the power of thoughts, everything is possible if a human mind so desires as expression by the idiom 'Mind over matter'.

The word 'psychokinesis' refers to the power of moving physical objects with the power of one's mind. Thus, as a concept it signifies one kind of an extreme of the term 'mind over matter'. Psychokinesis is often used synonymously with that of 'telekinesis' especially in case of movies and informal discussions on such topics. The latter word was originated to denote the physical movements of objects due to spirits and ghosts. Later on, during the 19th century, when a lot if studies were undertaken and the involvement of human mind in this phenomenon were realized, 'psychokinesis' term was coined.

Two types of measurement and therefore two categories of the psychokinesis phenomena are micro and macro psychokinesis respectively. The first one refers to minute changes in matter that is perceptible only through scientific instruments. The second type on the other hand refers to larger movement that can be seen by anybody with the naked eyes.

Other than such extreme paranormal aspects, the phrase 'mind over matter' finds extensive use in the mind centric explanations in the arena of philosophy or spirituality as well especially when it comes to responsibility assumption.

Responsibility assumption says that you yourself are responsible for your own fate. An important part of personal growth studies, it proclaims that your life and what it come out to be is what your mind power has resulted in. Apart from this, concepts like the law of attraction or affirmations are also part of the new age spirituality that focuses around the concept of mind over matter.

According to the law of attraction, the power of visualization and affirmations can attract whatever you desire in your life into manifestation in reality. What you need to do is focus all your attention and concentration on this object of desire of yours, visualizing yourself attaining the same and affirming your subconscious mind.

Countless claimants to the power of psychokinesis exists in our world of which some can be mentioned in this point. Martin Caidin was the author of the 1972 novel Cyborg. He was able to move energy wheels kept on the tops of one table or more. The Israeli Uri Geller was known for his spoon bending abilities while Nina Kulagina, the Soviet psychic was known for her short films which she made demonstrating her psychokinetic abilities. Mention must be made of Felicia Parise, an American laboratory technician who could move matters like plastic pill containers, aluminum foil, compass needles etc with the power of her mind. While she first performed these spontaneously, it was only after several intense concentration sessions and inspiration from the Nina Kulagina films that she was able to develop her powers to work at her will. At the height of her career was also featured as the First American to Move Matter with Mind by the tabloid National Enquirer. She retired after reporting bodily stress from psychokinesis demonstrations.

Coming to more remote places of the world and talking about the psychokinetic ability existence there that may not be easily researchable by scientific means, mention must be made of Himalayas, the great mountain range in India which is known as the centre of positive energy and spirituality of the ancient East. Rare individuals, sadhus and monks renounce the whole world and live here in the pursuit of the highest form of self-realization.

In the famous pilgrimage in India named normal 'kumbh mela' (annual), ardh kumbh mela (once in six years) and purna kumbha mela (once in twelve years), visitors can see such 'sadhus' come to River Ganges and perform such miraculous feats like psychokinesis and the like. Hence, it can be safely said that human mind has the power to do anything in life and achieve the impossible. You can move object with your thoughts or attract your object of desire with your concentration and in fact create, control and change anything that you want in the world by truly believing and having faith in the statement 'mind over matter'.

How Do You Explain Power of Mind?

As the college fund commercials back in the 80s said, 'the mind is a terrible thing to waste'. The commercial wasn't really about what we're going to be talking about here, but the idea is one which can be applied here as well.

Your mind has lot more power than you might think; and the power of mind is indeed a terrible thing to waste. When you can access the power your mind contains, you can use it to change the world around you for the better.

Have you heard about the Law of Attraction? In the last so many years it has been a popular topic that has transformed the live of several people around the world. When you think about things, you attract them to you—whether you do so consciously or not. This is the power of mind. Scientifically it has been proved that if we really work our mind, life will reap the fruits of betterment and prosperity. Medical science regards this as Placebo Effect and we should always remember the old saying 'Mind over matter'. This really points out that our mind can in fact can make things happen which ultimately matters in the long-run.

It has been scientifically proved that people really can think themselves well and of course the opposite is true as people can think themselves ill.

For example, how many times has your alarm gone off, or you had something happen that put you in a foul mood, and you've said 'Oh, great. It's going to be one of those days...', only to drag yourself into one bad experience after another, with each one compounding the ill will of the former?

It is not coincidence, if there is one thing that you should know by now everything happens for a reason. The reason is your mind.

What you will find is that it all revolves around quantum physics. This teaches us that you can create energy around you for anything. Even if we take it a little further, the way it works is your mind creates reality. So if you believe you're going to get in a car accident, and you keep telling yourself you will, then it's going to happen. However, we want you to train your mind to work towards the positive things in your life.

Many scientists now believe that all so called 'supernatural' powers such as extrasensory perception, telepathy, remote viewing, psychic and clairvoyant phenomena can be explained in terms of quantum theory. Even though many of us believe this to be phony television, it's actually part of the quantum physics theory. In short, nothing is solid and instead energy that is created by our minds.

If you could use the power of your mind to make the universe work with you rather than against you, wouldn't you want to learn how? There are a few techniques which can help you to do just that; keep reading to learn more about these methods.

Initially there must be a goal set in our mind and it must be done in a scrupulous way. The goal however should not contain anything that is not clear. If it is a amount of money that we have set in our mind, the amount must be clearly etched in our thoughts. After this we must drive all our thoughts and mind activities to this goal and will soon see the result.

It is very important that you are consistent. It has to be done all the time. You must remain focused and try to ignore all of the distractions which you are bound to get.

The sign of someone who's goal focused is that they're very driven. They work each and every moment towards some goal, rather than frittering their time away in unstructured pursuits. When they're working on a goal, they're driving towards it, rather than do it a little bit, then get distracted by something else.

Suppose that there's a house that is just perfect for you—but it's not even for sale and you're not ready to buy a home at the moment. However, the power of the mind can make it all happen.

Just think if you walked outside today and said, 'I'm going to buy my dream home within a few months.' It sounds good, it probably felt good to say it, but can you visualize yourself doing the work that it takes to get that dream house? This is a common mistake that most people overlook, but if you can picture yourself doing it, then it will be so.

Everywhere we go, our thoughts must be converge on the goal set. It may be the mortgage or the paints and our energies should also work in same lines. By focusing on this goal and putting your mental energy towards your objective, you can make it happen—don't be too surprised when your dream home goes on the market and your offer is accepted; and you even get just the right mortgage. It is the power of the mind which has made this come about, not simply good luck. The point is you need to take control. You need to decide for yourself that having the right affirmations everyday will change your life for the better. If you can do this, you can accomplish anything.

Secret Powers of Mind

Your mind has lot more power than you might think; and the power of mind is indeed a terrible thing to waste. When you can access the power your mind contains, you can use it to change the world around you for the better.

You might have noted that when you think about something, you will attract it to you. So keep that in mind as we get deeper into the subject. In a way, you can see this effect of mind power at work in clinical trials where it is known as the placebo effect. It's all about mind over matter. When you think about something; rather, when you believe in something, the power of the mind can make it happen.

Undoubtedly you have seen people 'think' themselves sick, and you have seen them 'think' themselves well. Our mind power is incredible. For example, how many times has your alarm gone off, or you had something happen that put you in a foul mood, and you've said "Oh, great, it's going to be one of those days...", only to drag yourself into one bad experience after another, with each one compounding the ill will of the former? It's actually the power of the mind that causes this to happen.

If you has ever studied the laws of quantum physics, you will know that there really is no such thing as 'matter'. At subatomic levels everything is pure energy and matter only exists because we are observing it. It is thought by some scientists that many of the phenomena we have always thought of as supernatural (such as remote viewing, telepathy and the like) are actually perfectly natural and explainable phenomena, though science may be a few years away from understanding the precise mechanisms behind them. On the extreme end, this leads to solipsism, the belief that nothing is real until you observe it, and the question of 'If a tree falls in the woods, and nobody's around, does it make any sound?' You've probably already experienced this a time or two without even realizing it. Maybe you were cutting out coupons and that inner voice told you if you don't stop you'll end up cutting your hand. Then of course, you didn't listen to this nonsense and all of the sudden you stick your other hand with the scissors. Granted, it may not have happened exactly like this, but you get the idea.

Lets see how you can use your mind power to get whatever you want out of life.

Initially there must be a goal set in our mind and it must be done in a scrupulous way. The goal however should not contain anything that is not clear. If it is a amount of money that we have set in our mind, the amount must be clearly etched in our thoughts. After this we must drive all our thoughts and mind activities to this goal and will soon see the result.

Once the goal is set, focus your mental actions on achieving that goal. Keep the effort constant; don't do it in bursts and lags.

There are people who understand the power of their mind. They work each and every moment very steadily towards what it is they want to achieve. They direct every action and every thought in that direction.

Suppose that there's a house that is just perfect for you—but it's not even for sale and you're not ready to buy a home at the moment. However, the power of the mind can make it all happen.

Suppose we put the theory of the power of the mind to test. We set a goal that we need to have a dream home and then completely become obsessed with the idea of buying such a house. We think about it day and night and even decide the colors of the walls and the other intricacies of the dream house.

Everything you do from now on needs to be focused on getting that dream house. You could visit the local Home store to choose the colour paint you want. You can look at getting the best rate mortgage.

Amazingly, your dream home then comes on the market. Again as if by a miracle events change so that you can afford to get the mortgage. All of the energy you directed to getting it has finally paid off!

This is within your grasp. You can do it—stop letting life happen to you, and you start happening to your life. Make your mind your most powerful asset, and you'll be astonished at the changes you can make in your life by setting small goals and focusing on them.

HOW TO SUCCESSFULLY PRACTISE POWER OF MIND?

The power of mind is in fact the most powerful thing in the universe and you can utilize your own mind power to create the life you want.

Your mind will manifest whatever you think about. What most people don't realize is that this happens whether you actively make it happen or not. So start to use the power of mind consciously and choose the life you want!

In a way, you can see this effect of mind power at work in clinical trials where it is known as the placebo effect. It's all about mind over matter. When you think about something; rather, when you believe in something, the power of the mind can make it happen.

It really is true that people can 'think' themselves better. Conversely they can 'think' themselves ill. It is just one of the many ways we can prove how powerful the subconscious mind can alter your life. Have you ever got up in the morning and decided that it was going to be a dreadful day and that is what happened? It is actually the power of the mind that causes this to happen.

Believe it or not there has been a huge amount of scientific evidence over the years. In fact everything can be explained in terms of quantum physics. Experiments show that there is no such thing as matter—everything is energy. And incredibly energy can only exist if someone is observing it. This means energy only exists because of the power of mind!

We as individuals never really give it a thought of how to actually use our mind power for the betterment of our lives. However this act in fact will prove healthier since if we do put our mind to good use, we will ultimately be able to achieve all that we desire in life. Moreover it is really a good practice to use our assets to enhance the way we live our lives.

There are ways that can be used so the power of the mind can be unleashed to achieve all that we want in our lives.

If you want to use the power of the mind to accomplish something, it's best to have a specific goal; for example, if you'd like to become wealthy, set your mind on a specific amount instead of being well off in general.

If you'd like to become financially well off, you need to focus on a specific amount rather than trying to focus on being wealthy in general. This makes it far easier for your mind to focus on this objective.

Of course, many people already know all about their own mind power. Whenever they want anything they focus on what they want and keep working on their goal physically and mentally until they have achieved it.

You have to make it happen and it all starts with the thought process. The first time around you'll probably have a hard time focusing on just one thought with a million racing through your head.

So make the decision to completely change your life by changing the way your subconscious mind constructs reality. Now say for example you want your dream home. You want it so much that it is almost an obsession. Your thoughts are filled with it all the time. Imagine yourself painting the master bedroom and landscaping the gardens.

Everything you do from now on needs to be focused on getting that dream house. You could visit the local Home store to choose the colour paint you want. You can look at getting the best rate mortgage.

Then as if by magic your dream home comes onto the market at a price you can afford. Somehow everything just comes together and it is yours! So everything you did, all of the energy that you directed at getting that house has paid off.

Every one of us can do this. It's just a matter of understanding your own inherent abilities and believing in the power of the mind to achieve the things you want out of life. Start with a small goal and you can work from there to accomplish ever greater things.

2

POSITIVE LIVING WITH MIND POWER

Your habits, the things you do everyday, are hard wired to the subconscious mind power. Old habits are harder to break because they're connected to the subconscious mind. To change those habits you need to begin working with mind power, and redirecting the subconscious mind power to create the new habits you want.

You can apply mind power by pushing yourself to do things differently everyday as often as you can. This means working with mind power in this way more than once a day. You should create new habits or work on new habits at least 7 or 8 times a day.

Mind power works with repetition. Through this repetition the subconscious mind power picks up the habit and then compels you to follow it. So it's important to decide what new habits you want to form and you should focus on creating habits that lead to success. Think about what habits you feel would help you succeed. In most cases simply getting more done in the same amount of time would leant do greater success. Making the right decisions also helps. As you focus on developing habits for success you begin to tap into the power of the mind and subconscious mind. When you back up what you think about with actions, you program the subconscious mind power to create the success you want. This is how mind power works. But remember, you have to work with this process repeatedly and keep directing the subconscious mind power everyday. So you have to push yourself to create new habits for success. This process works and to develop the mind power to make it last and to plant the new habit on the subconscious mind you need to work with the new habit for at least 30-days. Then it becomes a daily habit.

PRACTISING A POSITIVE LIFESTYLE

Let's face it most of us would love to live a life where everything just seems to go at a nice fluid pace with little or no interruptions or few setbacks. This would be great—and it can be done if you start practising a positive lifestyle.

How to Achieve a Positive Lifestyle?

This involves looking at things a little differently. It requires that you see and understand the positive aspects of people and situations—instead of just focusing on the negative aspects.

Too often we get caught up with the negative opinions, attitudes, actions and thoughts of those around us—and in the end we create a negative lifestyle that leaves us unhappy, depressed, hopeless and angry.

So, in order to avoid falling into this trap or in order to move from a negative lifestyle to a positive lifestyle—we need to begin changing the way we see things and change the way we interact with each other.

Change Your Negative Responses

The first thing you can do is to change your negative responses when dealing with people. For example, if someone asks you; "How are you." Instead of responding by saying: "Not bad." Why not say: "I'm doing great." Think about it for a second. Your first response was Not Bad, or I'm okay, or so-so—or hanging in there, or trying to get through the day—these are all negative statements that create more negative energy and perpetuate the negative lifestyle. Switching to the positive—to what you want—leads to creating more positive energy and a more positive attitude. If you actually start saying that you're doing great—in time you'll begin to believe it and your reality will reflect that—things will actually improve.

So when you're talking to other people—change your negative statements to positive comments. If you're in a conversation where everybody is just being negative—try saying something positive and see what happens. Watch the response—you'll be surprised at some of the things that happen. Some people may think your crazy—but a lot of people will actually start to see things differently. You'll actually get them to stop being so negative—and without knowing it—those very same people will begin looking at things in a more positive way. This may not happen the first time, and it may not happen all the time—but the more you do it—the more often you'll get them to focus on the positive events.

Focus on the Good Qualities

Often people will do things to make you uneasy, upset you, anger you—or just simply get under your skin. When this happens—it's okay to initially react—but after you've calmed down—look at the positive qualities in that person. Too often we focus solely on a person's negative qualities—and forget the good things. I've actually had people tell me that they can't think of anything nice about their co-workers, bosses, mother in-law, etc. This is a little hard to believe and what it shows is that the person is so caught up in living a negative lifestyle they can't see anything positive in anyone. It's like living in darkness for so long that now they forgot what impact light could have.

By looking at the positive you get your mind to shift it's attention—it now begins to see things differently and thus sends a different message and different energy to your subconscious. This new positive energy and positive message is picked up by your subconscious, your spirit and your higher power—they all bring positive situations to you. It's that old saying: "what goes around comes around." You focus on the positive in other people and other people will see the positive qualities in you. You focus on the good things in other people, and other people will see the good things in you and you'll attract positive situations in your life.

I'm not asking you to be a doormat and I'm not asking you to simply look at the positive qualities when someone is being unkind to you. Instead, I'm suggesting that you take a look at the positive qualities in addition to everything else. Don't neglect the positive qualities that a person has. Here's an example: Let's say you're taking your son or daughter to a basketball game. You're in the line and the guy behind you, who is also with his child, starts pushing. You ask him to back off and he gets angry—perhaps starts yelling and screaming—all of this is taking place in front of your child and his child. Finally, things calm down—you go to your seat and he goes to his. Perhaps you're still angry and silently cursing him as you sit in your chair. But can you see anything positive in that person? Most people would say no. But at least he was trying to spend some time with his kid. At least he took time out of his schedule, just like you did and took his kid to a game—just like you did. You don't know anything else about the person—but you just found some positive qualities.

When you do this you also release the anger and unhappiness—because you get your mind to focus on something positive instead of something negative—thus creating more positive energy. Try doing this with people you know and don't know.

Encourage the Positive

Another thing you can do is to be encouraging and positive—not just when you're talking to people—but go the extra distance to help someone out when you can. Offer encouragement when people have questions or concerns. Instead of shooting somebody down, or sharply criticizing them—take the high road—and see how much more of an impact a few words of encouragement will help. Listen to what people say and try to offer a positive suggestion to help in their situation.

When you do this you get your mind to go in a positive direction—which in turn will attract more positive situations—and you also back it up with action. It doesn't hurt to help people when they need a hand, a few words of encouragement will go a lot further than some harsh criticism.

Try Smiling

Finally, try smiling. It's actually a lot easier than frowning. It's true. Researcher and scientists have found that you actually use fewer muscles to smile than you do when you frown. Try smiling more and you'll actually start to feel better. Take some time to laugh at yourself and at things you find funny. Be a kid every once in a while—don't take things too seriously—after all having fun frees the soul and eases the mind. Do things you enjoy and you'll start creating a positive lifestyle.

These are just some of the things you could do to start living a positive lifestyle and attract more positive energy into your life. Once you start doing some of the things life will start to move at a more positive, fluid pace—and there won't be as many bumps along the road.

POSITIVE MENTAL ATTITUDE AND HAPPINESS IN LIFE

A positive mind anticipates happiness, joy, health and a successful outcome of every situation and action. Whatever the mind expects, it finds. Not everyone accepts or believes in positive thinking. Some consider the subject as just nonsense, and others scoff at people who believe and accept it. Among the people who accept it, not many know how to use it effectively to get results. It seems that many are becoming attracted to this subject, as evidenced by the many books, lectures and courses about it. This is a subject that is gaining popularity.

Positive and negative thinking are both contagious. All of us affect, in one way or another, the people we meet. This happens instinctively and on a subconscious level, through thoughts and feelings transference, and through body language. People sense our aura and are affected by our thoughts, and vice-versa. Is it any wonder that we want to be around positive people and avoid negative ones? People are more disposed to help us if we are positive, and they dislike and avoid anyone broadcasting negativity. Negative thoughts, words and attitude bring up negative and unhappy moods and actions. When the mind is negative, poisons are released into the blood, which cause more unhappiness and negativity. This is the way to failure, frustration and disappointment.

In order to turn the mind toward the positive, inner work and training are required. Attitude and thoughts do not change overnight. The power of thoughts is a mighty power that is always shaping our life. This shaping is usually done subconsciously, but it is possible to make the process a conscious one. Even if the idea seems strange give it a try, as you have nothing to lose, but only to gain. Ignore what others might say or think about you, if they discover that you are changing the way you think.

Always visualize only favourable and beneficial situations. Use positive words in your inner dialogues or when talking with others. Smile a little more, as this helps to think positively. Disregard any feelings of laziness or a desire to quit. If you persevere, you will transform the way your mind thinks.

Once a negative thought enters your mind, you have to be aware of it and endeavour to replace it with a constructive one. The negative thought will try again to enter your mind, and then you have to replace it again with a positive one. It is as if there are two pictures in front of you, and you choose to look at one of them and disregard the other. Persistence will eventually teach your mind to think positively and ignore negative thoughts. In case you feel any inner resistance when replacing negative thoughts with positive ones, do not give up, but keep looking only at the beneficial, good and happy thoughts in your mind. It does not matter what your circumstances are at the present moment. Think positively, expect only favorable results and situations, and circumstances will change accordingly. It may take some time for the changes to take place, but eventually they do. Another method to employ is the repetition of affirmations. It is a method which resembles creative visualization, and which can be used in conjunction with it.

Positive thinking brings inner peace, success, improved relationships, better health, happiness and satisfaction. It also helps the daily affairs of life move more smoothly, and makes life look bright and promising. People around you pick your mental moods and are affected accordingly. Think about happiness, good health and success, and you will cause people to like you and desire to help you, because they enjoy the vibrations that a positive mind emits. In order to make positive thinking yield results, you need to develop a positive attitude toward life, expect a successful outcome of whatever you do, but also take any necessary actions to ensure your success.

Effective positive thinking that brings results is much more than just repeating a few positive words, or telling yourself that everything is going to be all right. It has to be your predominant mental attitude. It is not enough to think positively for a few moments, and then letting fears and lack of belief enter your mind. Some effort and inner work are necessary.

- Are you willing to make a real inner change?
- Are you willing to change the way you think?
- Are you willing to develop a mental power that can positively affect you, your environment and the people around you?

Here are a few actions and tips to help you develop the power of positive thinking:

- Always use only positive words while thinking and while talking. Use words such as, 'I can', 'I am able', 'it is possible', 'it can be done', etc.
- Allow into your awareness only feelings of happiness, strength and success.
- Try to disregard and ignore negative thoughts. Refuse to think such thoughts, and substitute them with constructive happy thoughts.
- In your conversation use words that evoke feelings and mental images of strength, happiness and success.
- Before starting with any plan or action, visualize clearly in your mind its successful outcome. If you visualize with concentration and faith, you will be amazed at the results.
- Read at least one page of inspiring book every day.

— Watch movies that make you feel happy.
— Minimize the time you listen to the news and read the papers.
— Associate yourself with people who think positively.
— Always sit and walk with your back straight. This will strengthen your confidence and inner strength.
— Walk, swim or engage in some other physical activity. This helps to develop a more positive attitude.

Think positive and expect only favourable results and situations, even if your current circumstances are not as you wish them to be. In time, your mental attitude will affect your life and circumstances and change them accordingly.

USING POSITIVE ATTITUDE TO MANIFEST HAPPINESS

Positive attitude brings optimism into your life, and makes it easier to avoid worry and negative thinking. If you adopt it as a way of life, it will bring constructive changes into your life, and makes them happier, brighter and more successful. With a positive attitude you see the bright side of life, become optimistic and expect the best to happen. It is certainly a state of mind that is well worth developing and strengthening.

Positive attitude manifests in the following ways:

a. Positive thinking.

b. Constructive thinking.

c. Creative thinking.

d. Expecting success.

e. Optimism.

f. Motivation to accomplish your goals.

g. Being inspired.

h. Choosing happiness.

i. Not giving up.

j. Looking at failure and problems as blessings in disguise.

k. Believing in yourself and in your abilities.

l. Displaying self-esteem and confidence.

m. Looking for solutions.

n. Seeing opportunities.

A positive attitude leads to happiness and success and can change your whole life. If you look at the bright side of life, your whole life becomes filled with light. This light affects not only you and the way you look at the world, but also your whole environment and the people around you. If it is strong enough, it becomes contagious.

A positive attitude:

a. helps to achieve goals and attain success.

b. helps to achieve success, faster and more easily.

c. provides more happiness.

d. provides more energy.

e. provides greater inner power and strength.

f. provides the ability to inspire and motivate yourself and others.

g. provides the ability to surmount any difficulty.

If you have been exhibiting a negative attitude and expecting failure and difficulties, it is now the time to change the way you think. It is time to get rid of negative thoughts and behaviour and lead a happy and successful life. Why not start today? If you have tried and failed, it only means that you have not tried enough.

To developing a positive attitude that will lead you to happiness and success:

a. Choose to be happy.

b. Look at the bright side of life.

c. Choose to be and stay optimistic.

d. Find reasons to smile more often.

e. Have faith in yourself and in the Power of the Universe.

f. Contemplate upon the futility of negative thinking and worries.

g. Associate yourself with happy people.

h. Read inspiring stories.

i. Read inspiring quotes.

j. Repeat affirmations that inspire and motivate you.

k. Visualize only what you want to happen.

l. Learn to master your thoughts.

m. Learn concentration and meditation.

People with a positive frame of mind think about possibilities, growth, expansion and success. They expect happiness, health, love and good relationships. They think in terms of 'I can', 'I am able', and 'I will succeed'. True positive thinking is not just saying that everything will be okay, as a lip service, and at the same time think about failure. In order to bring beneficial changes and improvement into your life, positive thinking has to become your predominant mental attitude throughout the day. It has to turn into a way of life.

MIND POWER BEYOND POSITIVE THINKING

Mind power is beyond positive thinking. Once you realize that it is your power of thought—your thoughts and beliefs—that manifest your reality, you will want to pay close attention to the thoughts you are thinking.

Mind power is a straightforward, effective system based on the power of thought and the power of your subconscious mind. Mind power is a self-help programme for self-improvement that teaches you how to use affirmations, visualization, and the many other techniques that will aid you in harnessing the power of your subconscious mind.

Mind powers will help you develop the personal power that you already possess to create success and fulfilment in life. If you want to make changes in your life, you must look to the cause, and the cause is the way you are using the conscious mind—the way you are thinking.

You cannot think both negative and positive thoughts at the same time. One or the other must dominate. The mind is a creature of habit, so it becomes your responsibility to make sure that positive emotions and thoughts constitute the dominating influence in your mind.

In order to change external conditions, you must first change the internal. Most people try to change external conditions by working directly on those conditions. This always proves futile, or at best temporary, unless it is accompanied by a change of thoughts and beliefs.

Awakening to this truth, the way to a better, more successful life becomes crystal clear. Train your conscious mind to think thoughts of success, happiness, health, prosperity, and to weed out fear and worry. Keep your conscious mind busy with the expectation of the best, and make sure the thoughts you habitually think are based upon what you want to see happen in your life.

Water takes the shape of whatever container holds it, whether it be in a glass, a vase or a river bank. Likewise, your subconscious will create and manifest according to the images you habitually project upon it through your daily thinking. This is how your destiny is created. Your life is in your hands, to make of it what you choose from.

UNDERSTAND THE SUBCONSCIOUS MIND

In order to understand how the conscious and subconscious minds work together as a team to create your reality, let me again use an analogy. Your subconscious mind is like fertile soil that accepts any seed you plant within it. Your habitual thoughts and beliefs are the seeds which are being constantly sown within, and they produce in your life what is planted just as surely as corn kernels produce corn. You will reap what you sow. This is a law.

The conscious mind is the gardener. It is our responsibility to be aware of and choose wisely what reaches the inner garden. But unfortunately for most of us our role as gardener has never been explained to us. And in misunderstanding our role, we have allowed seeds of all types, both good and bad, to enter our inner garden.

The subconscious will not discriminate. It will manifest failure, ill health and misfortune just as easily as success and abundance. It works to reproduce in our life according to the seeds we have nurtured within. Your subconscious accepts what is impressed upon it with feeling and emotion whether these thoughts are positive or negative. It does not evaluate things like your conscious mind does, and it does not argue with you.

Once you grasp the fact that your subconscious will bring to you whatever you need, and you begin working, daily projecting the thoughts and images of what you want, seemingly chance and fortuitous events will begin to happen to you. Your powerful inner collaborator, working with your instructions, will bring to you the people and circumstances you require to meet your goals.

"A thousand unseen hands," as Joseph Campbell describes them, will come to your aid. Synchronicity appears to the uninitiated to be coincidence or luck, but it is neither. It is simply the operation of natural laws which you have set in motion with your thoughts.

Let me explain how it works. Modern physics now sees the universe as a vast, inseparable web of dynamic activity. Not only is the universe alive and constantly changing, but everything in the universe affects everything else. At its most primary level, the universe seems to be whole and undifferentiated, a fathomless sea of energy that permeates every object and every act. It is all one. In short, scientists are now confirming what mystics, seers and occultists have been telling us for thousands of years—we are not separate but part of one giant whole.

We also now know that everything in the universe is made up of energy. The chair that you're sitting on is comprised of energy. The walls of the room that you are now in, your computer, the events that happen to you are all made up of vibrations of energy. And our thoughts, too, are vibrations of energy. Our thoughts are of the same substance as the building blocks of the universe. Once we become aware of this remarkable fact, we can use it to our great advantage.

When, for example, you begin imprinting success upon your subconscious mind, it sets up a continuous vibration of energy that resonates upon the whole. The subconscious works day and night with this success vibration, attracting to you the people and circumstances necessary for your success. And remember that the subconscious will work equally hard to attract to you the circumstances necessary for your failure if that is how you habitually think.

We are fortunate that the laws of physical reality and the laws of the mind are now beginning to be understood. In past years, it might have seemed incredible that we could create our reality through this process, yet now, with these new insights, we understand how it works. Our thoughts being energy, it only makes sense that our repeated images, affirmations, visualizations, deeply held beliefs, fears and desires, vibrating within the larger web of reality, would have an affect upon that reality. In fact, when you stop and really think about it, since we are all connected, how could it be otherwise?

Mind Power gives you the tools to create a happy, successful and abundant life. Your destiny is yours for the making.

ELIMINATING NEGATIVE THINKING

Eliminating negative thinking is not simply about having a good attitude or feeling good or being positive just for the sake of being positive, although all these things have their benefits. It goes much deeper than that. The student of Mind Powers recognizes that thoughts are real forces and that how we think directly affects the things that happen to us. Our mind is like a garden, and we are the master gardeners. Through care and diligence we can create a botanical masterpiece, or through neglect our garden can be a mass of weeds—negatives, insecurities and failures. Understanding this, it becomes our duty and responsibility to eliminate negative thinking.

Some excellent techniques for eliminating negatives from your mind are provided below. Each technique is separate and independent from the other. In fact, some of these techniques will seem contradictory, but each will be highly effective in dealing with negative thinking.

1. Cut It Off

With this technique, the instant you recognize that you

are thinking a negative thought, you end it. You don't argue with it, you don't analyze it, you don't defend yourself against it, you cut it off. The moment you recognize that you're thinking a negative thought, simply cut it off and insert a totally different thought into your mind. And the key here is the instant you recognize you're thinking a negative thought. So whenever you become aware of negative thinking, act immediately, cut it off and set a totally different thought into your mind.

2. Label It.

As soon as you recognize that you are thinking a negative thought, instead of cutting it off as you did with the first technique, label it. You say to yourself, "What is happening inside me now is that I am experiencing 'a negative thought.'" That's all it is, and you keep reminding yourself of that. You keep reminding yourself that "It's only a negative thought. It's only a negative thought."

3. Exaggerate the Thought into All Ridiculousness

The exaggeration technique is a great technique, but you must exaggerate it into ridiculousness. And the key word here is ridiculousness. Let's say that you're a salesperson and you're out making your sales calls and suddenly the thought comes to you, "Ah, what's the use, I'm not going to make another sale today." And then you catch yourself and you say, "Wait a second that's a negative thought." With the exaggeration technique, what you might then say is, "That's right, I'm not going to make another sale today. Negatives come disguised as apparently real problems, or quietly, slipping in when we're not paying attention. And if we're not aware of the fact that our mind is the great trickster, forever conjuring up negative thoughts, then we'll buy into every single destructive thought that occurs to us. But with these techniques we have ways of dealing with negatives. That's why they are so valuable.

4. Counteract the Negative with the Exact Opposite

Whatever the negative is saying to you, you counteract it by thinking the exact opposite thought. When the negative thought comes to you: "I'm not going to make another sale today," you counteract it with, "I'm going to make several more sales today." When the negative thought comes to you, "I'm never going to get ahead financially," you counteract it with the exact opposite—"I'm going to be tremendously successful financially." When the thought comes to you, "I'm never going to have a meaningful relationship," you counteract it with the exact opposite—"I'm soon going to have a fabulous relationship."

You see, the mind can think only one thought at a time. It might seem to you that you're thinking many thoughts at a time, but what is actually happening is you're thinking one thought after another one thought after another one thought, and so on. At any given moment, you're only thinking one thought. So if you take out the negative and put in the exact opposite, you are taking the power away from that negative. Don't feed the beast. This is often exactly opposite to what most people do. Most people, when they have something that they don't want to have happen to them, they think about it, they worry about it, they focus on it, eventually they manifest it.

5. Use Affirmations on the Negative

If you don't know what affirmations are, they are simply statements that you repeat to yourself, over and over and over again. Affirmations are extremely effective, especially on those reoccurring negatives, the ones that have haunted you for years. What you do is the next time that you find yourself thinking that negative, calmly inform it that, "From here on, every time that you come to me, you will be met with two minutes of affirmations stating the precise opposite of what you are saying." And keep to that promise. So when your mind comes up with a negative such as, "I'm never going to get ahead in my life," as soon as that thought comes to you, counteract it with two minutes of affirmations stating the exact opposite: "I'm going to be tremendously successful in my life. I'm going to be tremendously successful in my life. I'm going to be tremendously successful in my life." And repeat this affirmation to yourself over and over again for the full two minutes. And if the negative comes back, hit it again with another two minutes.

These are five excellent ways of dealing with negative thinking. Use whichever ones you find beneficial, use them in combinations with one another, but most importantly, use them. Because you no longer need to be overpowered by negatives. No longer do you have to let these negatives bring you down. From this point on you possess the tools and techniques to eliminate negatives.

3

ACHIEVING SUCCESS WITH MIND POWER

With minor or day-to-day goals, one usually knows what he or she wants to do or get, but when it comes to major goals, most people don't know what they really desire. They desire to do something big, but they don't know what. They might have a vague idea, but this is not enough. The mind plays an important role in achieving every kind of success and goal, minor, everyday goals or major goals.

To accomplish anything, and to use your mind power, you have to know exactly what it is you want to do. To focus your mind power on a goal, you need to have a clear and well defined goal. How do you go about that?

You have first to think or meditate, to find out what is it that you want to accomplish or gain. This might not be a simple step, and requires deep thinking, investigation and time. After discovering what you really want to accomplish, you need to come up with a plan for action. You need to know what you have to do first and how to proceed. All of this requires planning, which means using the power of the mind.

After deciding on a goal and coming up with a plan, you need to hold in your mind a clear mental image of your goal. You need to see it accomplished. This step requires that you use your imagination, which is another power of the mind. Not everyone can visualize clear mental images, but regular training of the imagination can do wonders. You may, for example, look at photos of what you want to achieve, and then close your eyes, and try to see it in your imagination. This will enhance your ability to visualize.

At this point you have to display patience, self-discipline and the power to persist in your efforts. This requires a one pointed mind.

Affirmations are another useful mental tool for achieving success. What you affirm sinks into the subconscious mind, becomes part of the subconscious mind, and consequently affects your behaviour and actions. If your affirmations are positive, they lead you to success.

Another important power of the mind is thought transference. You need to be able to transmit your thoughts to other people, who would aid you with your plans. Often, you have to persuade others to invest in your plans or to help you in other ways. It is not enough just to talk with them, you need to believe in what you are saying; you need to be enthusiastic and persuasive, otherwise they won't listen and won't care. You need to be able to reject your and their doubts. To be able to do so, you need concentration, control over your thoughts, willpower, self-discipline and patience. All these are mental tools and skills.

Motivation is another mental and emotional power that you require for achieving success. How can you achieve anything if you are not motivated enough? To increase your motivation and enthusiasm, think often of your goal, about its advantages and benefits, and how it will change your life. Doing so, will strengthen your motivation.

Your thoughts, which are part of your mind, possess power. The thoughts that you most often think tend to come true. If you pour your mental energy into the same thoughts or mental images day after day, they will become stronger and stronger, and would consequently affect your attitude, expectations, behaviour and actions. These thoughts and mental images can even be subconsciously perceived by other people, who would then offer you help or opportunities. Your thoughts can also create what is usually termed as coincidence. They can attract into your life corresponding events, situations and opportunities.

Not every thought turns into reality. A thought has to be repeated often, and be tinged with desire, in order to come true. Doubts fears and worries tend to destroy what you build with the power of your mind. This means that you need to clear your mind from negative thoughts and doubts.

Understanding the mental power of the mind that you have and using it can bring you everything you want. Increasing mind power is something anyone can do. Your mind is your most precious asset yet most people treat it like it doesn't matter. Don't you make the same mistake.

Most don't even understand that the conscious mind and subconscious mind are two different things and the two don't always want the same things or even work together. If you can learn to understand how hypnosis works in your subconscious mind it's like having an owners manual for your own mind and you will be better able to use or increase your own mental power. You can easily learn this.

Scientists and doctors say we only use nine to eleven per cent of our brains or mental power. Just think how much better your life could be if you learned to use just five per cent more of your mental faculties.

POWER OF IMAGINATION

Imagination is the ability to form a mental image of something that is not perceived through the senses. It is the ability of the mind to build mental scenes, objects or events that do not exist, are not present or have happened in the past. Memory is actually a manifestation of imagination. Everyone possesses some imagination ability. In some it may be highly developed and in others it may manifest in a weaker form. It manifests in various degrees in various people.

Imagination makes it possible to experience a whole world inside the mind. It gives the ability to look at any situation from a different point of view, and enables one to mentally explore the past and the future.

It manifests in various forms, one of which is daydreaming. Though too much idle daydreaming may make one impractical, some daydreaming, when not being engaged in something that requires attention provides some temporary happiness, calmness and relief from stress.

In your imagination you can travel anywhere in the speed of light without any obstacles. It can make you feel free, though temporarily, and only in the mind, from tasks, difficulties and unpleasant circumstances.

Imagination is not limited only to seeing pictures in the mind. It includes all the five senses and the feelings. One can imagine a sound, taste, smell, a physical sensation or a feeling or emotion. For some people it is easier to see mental pictures, others find it easier to imagine a feeling, and some are more comfortable imagining the sensation of one of the five senses. Training of the imagination gives the ability to combine all the senses.

A developed and strong imagination does not make you a daydreamer and impractical. On the contrary, it strengthens your creative abilities, and is a great tool for recreating and remodeling your world and life.

This is a great power that can change your whole life. It is used extensively in magick, creative visualization and affirmations. It is the creator of circumstances and events. When you know how to work with it, you can make your hearts' desires come true.

Imagination has a great role and value in each one's life. It is much more than just idle daydreaming. We all use it, whether consciously or unconsciously, in most of our daily affairs. We use our imagination whenever we plan a party, a trip, our work or a meeting. We use it when we describe an event, explain how to arrive to a certain street, write, tell a story or cook a cake.

Imagination is a creative power that is necessary for inventing an instrument, designing a dress or a building, painting a picture or writing a book. The creative power of imagination has an important role in the achievement of success in any field. What we imagine with faith and feelings comes into being. It is the power beyond creative visualization, positive thinking and affirmations.

Visualizing an object or a situation, and repeating often this mental image, attracts the object or situation into our lives. This opens for us new, vast and fascinating opportunities.

This means that we should think only in a positive manner about our desires, otherwise we may create and attract into our lives events, situations and people that we don't really want. This is actually what most of us do, because we don't use the power of imagination correctly.

If you do not recognize the importance of the power of the imagination, and let it run riot, your life may not be as happy and successful as you would have wanted it to be.

Lack of understanding of the power of the imagination is responsible for the suffering, incompetence, difficulties, failures and unhappiness people experience. For some reason, most people are inclined to think in a negative way. They do not expect success. They expect the worst, and when they fail, they believe that fate is against them. This attitude can be changed, and then life will improve accordingly.

Understanding how to use your imagination correctly, and putting this knowledge into practice, for your own and others' benefit, will put you on the golden path to success, satisfaction and happiness.

Imagination and Inner Vision

Imagination, which can also be called inner vision, is a gift that has many positive applications, but more than often it is not well-developed or correctly used. Few people possess the ability to control what enters their minds. They let their minds and imagination do as they please, and let any stray thought or mental image appear on the screen of their inner vision. This lack of control leads to lack of control over their lives.

Let your imagination run riot, and your life will be a mess. Control it and visualize only what you intentionally decide to visualize, and you change your life in accordance with your will.

What is the imagination, the inner vision? It is the ability to see in one's mind mental images of something that exists, and also the ability to imagine objects, situations or circumstances that do not exist now. Imagination is not only visualizing mental images. It is possible to visualize using all the five senses. You can visualize a sound, taste, smell or a sensation.

If you watch your mind, you will find out that you are constantly using your imagination in various ways.

You use it while thinking about the past or future, planning, painting, writing, and describing something. You use it when you describe how to get to a certain street, when you read and when you daydream.

Do you write, paint or engage in any creative activity? Do you cook, decorate or love to do new things? If you do, then you are using your imagination.

When you worry or feel fear you use it too. At such times you automatically visualize unhappy or unfortunate situations. If you keep visualizing these negative mental images you may eventually attract them into your life.

If you see in your inner vision how you want your life to be, and continue watching this mental scene every day with faith, concentration and love, one day your life will look exactly as you imagine.

There are some people who say they have no imagination. There is no such thing. It may be weak, but they certainly possess it. It might also happen that their visual imagination is not strong, but they can visualize using their other five senses, as mentioned earlier.

The ability to visualize clearly can be developed, and this can be fun. Exercises for developing this ability will at the same time also improve your ability to concentrate, and as a bonus, you might find that you gain a power which you can use to shape and improve your life.

How to Developing Your Imagination?

To develop your Imagination power of your inner vision:

- Find some fifteen minutes every day for the exercises.
- Visualize something simple that you can believe you can get, such as going to a movie with your girl/boy friend or with your husband/wife, eating at

a certain restaurant or doing something else you would like to do.

- Visualize your desire clearly, and include in the visualization all the five senses. If it is watching a movie together with another person, imagine the two of you entering the cinema and sitting down. Listen to the people around you, use your sense of smell and feel the coldness or warmth in the cinema hall. Visualize eating popcorn or drinking some soft drink, and enjoy the taste and smell.
- You might find out it is easier to imagine with some of the senses, and a little difficult to imagine with the others. Go on with the exercises and you will strengthen your ability to imagine with all the senses.
- Do the same exercise everyday, and you will find that it gradually becomes easier.
- Sometimes you may find that your mind starts to verbalize about what you are imagining. Be careful not to replace the imagination with words. The aim is to use the imagination, not words.

If you follow these suggestions you will develop your imagination, the power of the inner vision, which will be useful to you in many situations. You might also be surprised to discover that what you see in your mind, in your inner vision, comes true in real life.

BECOMING THE MASTER OF THE MIND

Most people keep thinking the same kind of thoughts, and visualize the same mental images in an unconscious automatic manner. This means they keep viewing the same movie in their minds, and consequently, go on creating and living the same kind of life. You can change the thoughts and images in your mind, which is equivalent to inserting a new cassette into the VCR of the mind. As thoughts create events and circumstances, by changing the habitual thoughts, life's events and circumstances change too.

Most people don't know or don't believe that it is possible to change their way of thinking. The reality of this possibility has never occurred to them.

There are people who have the knowledge and make the effort. If they persist in their efforts to become more conscious of their thinking process, and attempt to control and filter the contents of their minds, they realize in a practical and direct way that their thoughts are creative and possess power.

Silencing the mind is a higher stage that very few know about it, and fewer take practical steps to achieve it. If and when one reaches this goal he realizes that he is not his mind or his thoughts, but something beyond. He realizes and experiences in a very clear and direct manner the reality of his True Essence, and the illusion of what is called "reality".

The ability of silencing the mind is the key to the switch of the mind, enabling us to turn it on and off as we wish. When we are able to switch it off at will, we experience serenity of mind, strength, confidence and happiness. When the mind and its thoughts are quiet, we are able to use the mind in a most effective way.

Silencing the thoughts and the incessant, tiring, consuming chatter of the mind makes us enjoy a peaceful and joyous consciousness. At this stage, we become the master of the mind.

Conquering the Mind

A strong power of concentration makes it easier to free the mind from thoughts. When there are no thoughts to distract, one becomes fully aware and conscious of the true eternal inner being. This is the goal of spiritual seekers, yogis and saints. This is the secret goal beyond every tradition and religion. This secret is yours to live and enjoy, if you strive towards it.

The mind is responsible for everything that happens. It is the creator of everything in the world. The world is dependent on the mind for its existence. When in deep sleep with no dreams, are you conscious of the world? Is someone in a swoon, conscious of the world? No, consciousness of the world happens only when the mind is active. In deep meditation, when the mind is quiet the world seems to disappear.

When you master your mind, you master your world. When you are able to silence the mind, you free yourself of negative habits and attitudes. Then the mind cannot influence the way you feel, your moods, and your behaviour.

When you can silence the mind, at least for a while, you realize that you are not the mind. It is a sort of energy that occupies your attention incessantly. For someone who encounters this approach for the first time, it may sound weird and silly. Someone who has practiced meditation for some time, or is conversant with the Eastern philosophies will understand and accept these words. From this inner silence, you can look at the mind, understand what it is, and come to know its nature and how and why it works.

While working towards this inner state, the mind usually suggests all kinds of reasons and excuses why it is better not to bring it under control. It wants to be free and roam wherever it likes. It believes that if it is silenced, life will cease to be. It cannot accept that life can go on without its incessant chatter and inner dialogues. It is false logic, as the mind cannot know what is beyond it. The moment it is silenced it does not participate in what happens after this silence. Then how can it experience a state in which it is absent? It cannot think about a state it has never experienced.

There is no vacuum in nature. When the mind is made quiet, something "new" steps in. It is the Universal Consciousness, Spirit, the creative power, your "inner I". You can call it whatever you want. It is a power that has always existed, and it is in us, it is us. It is our true Consciousness, which we have forgotten.

Power of Thoughts

If you keep thinking about difficulties, fears and failure your life will mirror these thoughts. If you keep thinking about your current circumstances you will keep recreating them. Most people get caught in this way of thinking, and consequently, attract into their lives the same kind of events and circumstances over and over again.

You can change your thoughts and choose the thoughts you want. This will change your life. You can right now start to think in a different way and paint new, beautiful, and positive images in your mind. You can refuse to look at the old pictures and scenes that fill your mind. You can look at the mental pictures of your choice, even if your actual circumstances are very different from these mental images.

You have a projection room in your mind, and you can choose which film to play. In the inner room of your mind, you can hang the pictures and paintings of your own choice. Does a feeling of power surge through you now, as you read these lines? You can master your life!

Thoughts are the inner strings that pull circumstances and situations. You can be the one pulling these strings and make your life happier and more satisfying. When you are the master of your mind you have the power to improve your inner and emotional life, relationships and your material and financial status.

Some make a mediocre change; some go to the extreme, and become leaders in politics, education, finance or any other field. Your ability, and how far you go is dependent on how free you are from being the slave of the mind and subject to its tyranny, and the extent of your ability to choose your thoughts and change the contents of your mind.

As mentioned earlier, it is possible to go even further than this, though few do. There are some who aspire to reach the source of the mind and find the switch that turns it on and off. This is the switch of true inner freedom. When they succeed, they realize the secret that many have sought down the ages. They find the silence beyond thoughts, the real freedom.

Becoming the boss of your mind enables you to think about what you want, when you want to. You stop being influenced by outside forces, and become a partner in the creation of your life. When you rise above your mind, you will be able to recognize it as it is, a tool for your use. You will arrive at a point, where you will be able to free yourself from its dictates. This may ultimately lead you to experience a higher state of consciousness, about which all the spiritual traditions of the world have always taught about, and towards which they pointed.

KNOW THE INNER POWERS

We all possess various inner powers, but they are often in a dormant state. In order to awaken these inner powers and start using them, special training and inner work is required. Sometimes, due to various unpredicted circumstances, some of these powers might manifest unexpectedly and temporarily.

What are these inner powers? Let's review them briefly?

The Power of Concentration

This is the ability of focusing the attention on one single object or thought, and at the same time excluding all other unrelated thoughts from the mind.

Concentrating on one single thought or subject directs the mental energies into one point and prevents their dissipation. Concentration strengthens the power of the thought focused on, and can achieve wonders. This action is similar to the action of a magnifying glass that concentrates the rays of the sun into one single beam, and which can then burn a piece of paper.

This ability can be developed through special exercises. Any time spent on such exercises is time well spent. The more time and energy you devote to strengthening the power of concentration, the stronger this ability becomes.

Willpower

This is the inner strength to make decisions, take action and handle and execute any aim or task, regardless of inner resistance, discomfort or difficulty. It manifests as inner firmness, decisiveness, determination, resolution and persistence.

Self-discipline

This inner power manifests as the ability to forgo instant gratification in favor of something better, and of the giving up of instant pleasure and satisfaction for a higher goal. It is the ability of the individual to stick to actions, thoughts and behaviour, and which leads to improvement and success.

Power of Imagination

This is the ability to experience a whole world inside the mind. Imagination is a creative power. By training and using it correctly one can create and attract health, wealth, happiness and favourable events and circumstances. A well developed and strong imagination does not make one a daydreamer or an impractical person. On the contrary, it strengthens the creative abilities, the ability to solve problems and is a great tool for recreating and remodeling one's life and circumstances.

Persistence

It is so easy to stop and give up when one's plans don't turn out as expected or take too much time to accomplish. Persistence manifests as the inner strength to continue in spite of difficulties, obstacles and failure.

Motivation

Motivation is an inner driving force, which directs one toward a chosen aim or goal. In order to accomplish anything, one needs a driving, directing power, otherwise nothing would happen, and motivation supplies this power.

Ambition

Wishful thinking is not strong enough to make one take action. A wish is a weak desire. Only a strong desire can drive one forward, to take action, follow plans and accomplish desires and goals.

Self-confidence

This is faith in one's abilities, strength and power. Confidence leads to courage, doing things, trying new things and to success.

Detachment

This is the ability to remain calm and uninvolved on the emotional and mental levels. This ability saves one a lot of trouble, discomfort, fears and worries. Detachment helps one to accept calmly what cannot be changed and go on with one's life. Detachment leads to inner balance and peace.

Peace of Mind

A peaceful mind is free from the compulsion of incessant and restless thinking and worrying. When thoughts do not disturb the tranquility of the mind one experiences inner happiness. A person possessing peace of mind is calm and in control of himself. Such a person retains inner balance under almost all conditions, and is hardly affected by negative circumstances and situations.

- *(a)* Can you imagine a successful person, who cannot concentrate on a task, hasn't the willpower to follow his or her goal or is unable to visualize the kind of success he or she desires to attain?
- *(b)* Can anyone reach high spiritual levels without concentration, willpower and self-discipline?
- *(c)* Even people who pursue psychic or occult training need the above-mentioned inner powers.
- *(d)* Do you wish to follow a particular course of action, change habits, lose weight, learn a new skill, study or succeed in your examinations?
- *(e)* Do you desire to develop psychic powers, clairvoyance or telepathy?
- *(f)* Do you want to excel in creative visualization?

Whatever is your aim in life is, all of the above mentioned inner powers are of great importance and should be developed and strengthened.

KNOW YOUR PSYCHIC POWERS

Every person displays or experiences some psychic power every now and then, though most often these experiences are dismissed as pure coincidence. You certainly have had some premonitions about something that was going to happen, dreams that came true, or you felt and knew what someone was thinking of you. These experiences often came spontaneously, suddenly, and without any prior preparations.

Some people are more naturally psychic from others, and psychic experiences are a more common occurrence with them. Sometimes they just accept the fact that they are a bit different from others in their perceptions, having as if a sixth sense, while others pursue the subject more deeply, reading, learning and searching for guidance. They try to develop these powers and bring them under their control.

Psychic powers can be developed through special training, even by people who are not naturally psychic. These are fascinating powers, which allow a trained person to peek beyond the material plane, and know things that remain hidden to other people.

There are several risks in using and developing psychic powers, which one has to take into account when developing them:

1. The knowledge gained can be used for selfish purposes.
2. The psychic could be wrong in interpretation of the experience, and might unintentionally mislead, misguide or cause harm to other people.
3. Some of the psychic powers requires one to be mentally passive, so as to be able to tune in to other minds, thus letting in some external powers, which might have a negative influence.

4. One who is not well-balanced and lacks self-control and discipline, might find it difficult to stop the psychic impressions and lead a practical normal life.
5. Pursuing psychic training might deter one from the path of self-improvement and spiritual growth, leading him or her to constant seeking of these perceptions and leading away from inner calmness and peace of mind.

If one desires to develop psychic powers, it would be wiser first to develop some concentration ability, control over the mind, willpower, self-discipline and mental and emotional detachment. This would ensure that one be able to open and close at will the mental doors, and so avoid being influenced by what he/she perceives. This will also reduce the danger that one might misuse the powers or get his/her ego inflated by them.

There are different kinds of psychic powers or gifts, as they are often called. Another term used is—extra-sensory perception (ESP). Here is a list of some of the psychic powers:

(a) *Clairvoyance* (clear vision)—Seeing far away scenes and places or hidden things, without using the physical eyes. Clairvoyance enables one to perceive scenes and mental images with the mind's eye.

(b) *Clairaudience* (clear hearing)—Perceiving sounds or words from a distant or from other realms. Clairaudience enables one to hear words and sounds not perceived by the physical ears.

(c) *Clairempathy* (clear emotion)—Sensing the attitude or emotions of another person.

(d) *Psychometry*—Perceiving information about a person, place or an object, by holding in one's hands an object belonging to the person or place. In

Psychometry one usually holds some small personal object such as a watch, ring, key or other personal object.

(e) *Psychokinesis*—The ability to move objects through the powers of the mind.

(f) *Intuition*—Perceiving an idea, knowledge or information directly. This is what is commonly called "a gut feeling". Intuition is some kind of inner knowledge and certainty about something.

(g) *Telepathy*—Reading other people thoughts and sending them your thoughts.

(h) *Mental influence*—An advanced kind of telepathy that allows one to influence the minds of other people.

(i) *Psychic healing*—The ability to cure pains or illnesses by transferring some kind of healing energy.

(j) *Auric sight*—The ability to see or sense the colors of the aura, and thereby understand certain things about the moods, emotions, thoughts or health of other people.

HOW TO STRENGTHEN YOUR MIND POWER?

The mind is extremely powerful. To strengthen your mind power we need to understand the mind and use effective mental programming to bring you greater success.

The brain can be categorized into three levels of consciousness; the conscious mind, the sub-conscious mind and unconscious mind. When programming on the mental level, all 3 levels must be aligned for the mental programming to succeed. I'm sure you have experienced a conscious intention or goal and it simply has not manifested or come to fruition. It is likely there is a subconscious and/or unconscious pattern blocking the success of your conscious intention. The key to success or failure is often unknown at the conscious level.

Let us explore this further to strengthen your mind power and success in mental programming.

The Conscious Mind

The conscious mind is everything that we are aware of; thinking, analyzing, learning, perceptions, and observations, storing experiences using our five senses; sight, smell, hear, touch and taste. The conscious mind is logical and linear and likes to understand why, where, when, how and what. The conscious mind is everything in our waking thinking state that we are consciously aware of or can easily bring into our awareness or thinking. Human beings operate from the conscious mind approximately 5% of the time. This is where we begin for mental programming.

1. Create a vision of a positive desired outcome.
2. Intensify the colours, sounds and feel of this desired outcome. The more colour, energy and excitement, the more energy for success.
3. Visualize this outcome as if it were now, see it, feel it, believe it.
4. Strengthen this visualization until you have a strong Yes feeling that it is so. Take as long as you need to see, feel, hear, believe in this outcome, You feel the certainty of this goal. A colourful, delightful, exciting goal.
5. Now that you have a strong, clear, certain vision of your goal, put this vibrant, colourful picture in a bubble and let it float into the future.
6. Now let go of that vision and let it be. It is done.

The Subconscious Mind

The subconscious mind stores our memories and is equipped to process and recall stored data. The subconscious mind is active during sleep and witnesses our dreams. The subconscious mind is actually a library of every image you have ever seen and will absorb and remember everything it is exposed to, whether you consciously register or not. The subconscious mind cannot tell the difference between what is real and what is imagined. Therefore, be mindful of what you allow into your consciousness.

The subconscious mind is where we hold our beliefs. The subconscious mind powers are far more powerful and respond faster than the conscious mind. Human beings operate from subconscious mind approximately 95% of the time.

Ensure your conscious desires and subconscious beliefs are 'in-sync' when programming mentally.

The Unconscious Mind

The unconscious mind is unlimited in time and space. The unconscious mind involuntarily moves parts of our body and operates our entire physiology. As human beings we are not aware of our unconscious mind, it appears to be at rest. The unconscious mind stores all knowledge (past, present and future) and is sometimes called the "collective unconscious." It is not limited to the experiences of one individual, it stores the data for all places, times, and experiences of all people, ie humanity.

The unconscious mind is all knowing (omniscience), all powerful (omnipotence), all creative (omnificence) and always present everywhere at the same time. It has also been called the Universal Mind or Mind of God which pervades the entire Universe. We are all connected to everything and everyone. In deep meditation you may access the collective unconsciousness and draw from universal wisdom and knowledge of the ages. Intuition also stems from the universal mind.

Step to Strengthening the Power of Mind

The first step to strengthening the power of your mind and successful mental programming is to check that your goal is aligned with your beliefs and thoughts on a conscious level.

Greater than 70% of most people's thoughts are negative or redundant. Positive thoughts bring a positive response; the placebo effect. One third of medical healing is due to the placebo effect. No thought or negative thoughts bring no result. This is the nocebo effect.

When you don't achieve your outcome or goal, that is a good indication your conscious and subconscious mind are not aligned. Your thoughts and beliefs are not aligned.

You now have two choices:

1. Change your conscious goal to align with your Soul; meditate or contemplate to get clear.
2. Access and resolve your subconscious and unconscious patterns and that may be holding you back from achieving your dreams

What are your deep beliefs? Does your belief system support your goal? You may not be readily aware of your beliefs. To explore your subconscious beliefs you can use meditation or self-hypnosis, as long as you can hold yourself in a space of awareness for the process. You can seek help from a practitioner that may use some of these very effective tools that uncover subconscious beliefs and unconscious knowing.

1. Hypnosis
2. Neurolinguistic programming
3. Time line therapy

4. Meditation/contemplation of enquiry
5. Emotional freedom technique
6. Theta healing
7. Rebirthing

and many more.

As each mental layer is purified, consciousness is gained and you become more powerful.

The power of your mind is strengthened and mental programming will be successful and instantaneous. There will be no limiting (subconscious) beliefs and there will be attunement with the universal mind, universal consciousness, collective consciousness.

HOW TO ACHIEVING YOUR DREAMS AND GOALS?

Achieving your dreams and goals depends on several factors:

1. You should have a specific goal.
2. You have to be sure that you really want to achieve your goal.
3. You need to have a clear mental image of your goal.
4. You need a strong desire.
5. You need to disregard and reject doubts and thoughts about failure.
6. Show confidence and faith and persevere until you gain success

How many people fulfil all the above-mentioned requirements? Just a few! Most people do not know that there are some laws governing success, which should be followed. It is so easy and simple to daydream and then say, "Well it is just a daydream. It will never come true". It is so easy to give up due to lack of faith.

Achieving your goals shouldn't be a tough ordeal. In fact, it can be fun and pleasure, if you go in the right way. It is not hard physical work that brings success. Great success does not require hard physical labor. In fact, you need to do mental work.

Visualization and repeating affirmations make up this mental work, and are important stepping stones to achieving success. When you visualize and affirm you focus and channel your energies toward your goal. Your mind is geared toward finding solutions to bring your goal into manifestation.

By thinking in a positive manner on your goal, and not letting any doubts enter your mind, your intuition starts working, you see opportunities, and you have energy at your disposal to follow your goals and dreams.

Some people listen to subliminal messages, for programming their minds for success. There are many CD's available today, which implant subliminal messages into the mind, so as to activate its power. Some people prefer to use them, because this does not require any effort on their part. It is said that these subliminal messages, which go straight to the subconscious mind, bring faster results. Maybe they do, but then you have no control on what goes into your mind.

When you visualize and affirm your goals, you gain much more then just programming your mind passively with subliminal messages. The attention, intention and energy you channel toward visualizing and affirming, develop in you inner strength, concentration, willpower and self-discipline. You actively develop your inner powers.

One of the advantages of visualization and affirmations is that you can use them wherever you are, at any time, without the necessity of any external instruments. All you need is your mind.

Success appears in various ways, sometimes in a miraculous way, sometimes in an ordinary way, and sometimes through an opportunity that appears. A door opens, but you have to get in and take advantage of the opportunity.

Correctly following these methods will bring you more ambition, inspiration and motivation, which would enhance your chances of success.

Remember, there are big goals and there are many small daily goals, which visualization and affirmations can make them easier and faster to achieve.

People often erroneously think that goals mean only big goals, such as:

— becoming wealthy,

— getting an expensive car,

— possessing a big house with a swimming pool,

— building a very successful business.

The truth is that the following are no less important goals:

— getting to work on time,

— spending more time with the family,

— reading a book,

— going to see a movie,

— eating less.

Like any other subject, if you want to do it right you need to study it right. It is simple and easy to learn to achieve success through visualization and affirmations. Anyone can learn to use them right.

10 Steps to Achieve Goals

1. *Be specific about what you want to achieve:* Most people don't know what they want to with their

life, and even after thinking hard, they often don't come with something they really want to do. This is one of the main reasons that in spite of so many books on success, most people live an average life, not achieving some major success.

2. *Draw up a plan of action:* Devote as much time as you need to find a goal or goals, even minor goals are okay. Not everyone really desires great success and is willing to completely change his/her life. Not everyone desires to be a millionaire, or possesses the talent to make money.

   After finding a goal that you really desire to achieve, draw up a plan or even several plans, and be as practical as possible.

3. *Make a list of steps:* List the steps you need to take, such as signing up for a course, studying, reading, developing the required skills, looking for a job, etc, and other steps you need to implement that will take you closer to achieving your goal.

4. *Act, do not be passive:* Take action and follow the steps on your list. Don't just wait for things to happen.

5. *Read and listen to advice:* Read books or articles about what you want to achieve. Meet people who can help you and listen to their advice, but use your common sense and reason before accepting anything.

6. *Alternative plans:* If a certain plan doesn't work, look for an alternative one.

7. *Examine your goals periodically:* Some goals aren't worth achieving. Circumstances and people change. Some goals lose their importance. It is a good idea to re-examine your goals regularly and weed out the worthless ones.

8. *Repeat affirmations:* Affirm with faith and feelings that your goal has already been achieved. If you don't undo your affirmations with doubts and lack of belief, they will be accepted by your subconscious mind, which will then provide you with more desire and motivation.
9. *Visualize your goal:* Visualization will also affect your subconscious mind, which will keep you motivated, focused on your goal, and more aware of ideas and opportunities.
10. *Take action:* Don't just affirm and visualize and do nothing. Take any action required to bring your goal into fruition. Follow your intuition, new ideas and opportunities that present themselves, and accept help from other people.

MANIFESTING SUCCESS WITH CONSCIOUSNESS

Your mind and consciousness are the creators of your life. The more conscious you are of yourself, the stronger you become. I do not mean being conscious of your body, ego or who you are as a person. I mean conscious of being conscious, of the feeling of existence, the feeling of being alive, not from the point of view of the physical body. It is the inner feeling and sensation that you exist as a spiritual entity. It is the awareness of your inner essence, as something beyond the body and the ego.

Consciousness is your essence. Without it you are non-existent. It gives your personality and your body the power to function. Because of it, you can walk, eat, work, study, talk and understand. It is this something that makes you feel alive. It is intangible, yet very real. It is your awareness of life, of being alive and existing.

When you focus your consciousness on success, and fill it with the feeling of success, things start happening.

When the certainty of success is saturated into the consciousness, you have a great power in your hands. Success consciousness means that you are certain of your success without doubts. Like the story about the faucet, you should have no doubts that you are going to get what you are thinking about.

Do you want a new job? Evoke feelings of certainty without doubts that you have already got it. Do you desire a wife, a husband, a vacation, promotion, a new car, or money? Do not entertain any doubts. Your consciousness should be focused and assured of success.

How can you attain success if your consciousness is focused on failure and doubts? Become aware of your consciousness, of the feeling that you *are existing and alive,* focus on it, and at the same time think of success, and you have a mighty power at your disposal.

Whatever it is that you desire to bring about, try to feel as if it has already happened. Re-live the happiness you experienced when you realized ambitions in the past, and transfer this happiness and the feeling of achievement into the present moment, and your success is assured. Feelings are very important for success. They are the current of power that brings success. They have to be living, strong, real and sincere feelings, in order to bring results. Feelings add fire and energy to a thought and make it strong. They are like the electric current, which makes instruments work.

Success consciousness is a state of inner certainty, even if your current reality is far from what you want it to be. It does not cost you money to experience it. Do not let doubts and contrary thoughts and feelings enter your mind, and you are on the way to success in what you do.

Evoke the certain feeling of success. Pour fuel into this feeling, and always keep it alive. It is a state of consciousness, intentionally invoked, even though the outer circumstances are to the contrary. Consciousness has the power to create. What is in the consciousness comes out in the end. There is nothing supernatural here, this is the way nature works.

It may take some time until Consciousness manifests your ambition and desire in the outer world. It should be saturated with the utter certainty of success, not with just a faint belief. There should be complete lack of doubts, and only great certainty. Under these circumstances magic is released into the air.

You may look at this process as if it is a game. Put aside your doubts for a while. Treat these inner actions in a spirit of a game, fun and challenge. This is a serious subject, but by having fun with it, you reduce your tension, and are enabled to put forth more energy in a positive manner. Enjoy this process, and you will be surprised at the outcome.

It is quite possible to put the focus on feelings and not only on thoughts. Feelings, if strong enough, cause things to happen, even if the related thought is only in the background. If the feelings and emotions are strong, and connected to an event or an object, this event or object becomes a fact. Those who have difficulty in visualizing pictures will certainly appreciate this approach.

Think about your life, and you will find out that there were times that you had a certainty about something, without really trying intentionally to bring it about, and that thing happened. It might have been something positive and good or something else that was to your detriment. If you accept and follow what you have read here, you will be able to use this ability consciously.

What you have read so far is actually about the power of creative visualization and thinking, but focusing more on feelings and consciousness, rather than on images and thoughts. Think about what you have read, and try to put it into practice. Let abundance and success enter your life.

THE RIGHT ATTITUDE TOWARD SUCCESS

If you examine your ambitions, desires and goals in a very sincere way, you may discover to your amazement that you have some fears of realizing them. You want something, but yet you are afraid to have it. You may wish for a different kind of life, but in your subconscious mind you fear the change. You may desire to get married, but you are afraid of marriage. You want to change your job, but you are afraid to make the change. This is because the familiar gives security. You can find many examples like these.

When you have a goal, and at the same time you experience doubts and fears, you are actually driving away the materialization of your dreams. It is like sailing against the wind and the currents; you are pushed back all the time. These fears hide at the back of the mind, and you may not be conscious of them. Analyzing any desire you have, and trying to find out if there is any resistance to bringing it about, will bring the fears into the open, and enable you to throw away your fears and inner brakes.

What will happen if you turn on the tap in your sink, what will you say? Do you just believe that water will flow out of it, or are you absolutely certain that water will flow out? Beliefs are not always based on facts, but on ideas and thoughts or on what we were taught to believe. Now you may ask, what has belief to do with the flow of water from the tap? You might be certain, with no doubts whatsoever that water is going to flow out from the tap in your kitchen when you open it. It is a sure thing. You take it for granted, and never even think about it. You are absolutely sure that water is going to flow out. The same should happen with respect to your ambitions and desires. You must regard them as feasible. More than that, you should consider them as real. When you daydream, you have to see and treat the dream as real, without any doubt.

Most people look at the world around them as something real and solid. Their minds are chained to what they see around; their thoughts reflect their life, circumstances and events. Rarely will someone disregard his surroundings and circumstances and create in his mind a different situation. Surroundings and environment influence people's life, and they regard them as something they can do nothing about. When you become able to see in your mind a different kind of life, you stop being enslaved by circumstances and start creating your own life.

Nobody becomes impractical, indifferent or weak, if he holds in his mind thoughts and images that are different and unrelated to his present life situation. It is possible to handle the affairs of life in the best way, and at the same time visualize and expect a different kind of reality. Use your imagination to see and feel in your mind a different situation or environment, and watch what happens.

If you go on thinking the same thought it will materialize, if your mind is not opposing and resisting it with negative thoughts, fears, worries and doubts.

Sometimes the materialization of your thought or desire may be delayed due to the fact that you are not yet ready for it. Maybe you need some more knowledge, training, or a new skill before you get what you want. Sometimes things happen suddenly in an unusual way, but most often they come in a natural, gradual manner.

Success Has Many Definitions

Everyone desires success in one form or another. Some just daydream about it, while others do something to achieve it. What does success mean to you?

Here are some definitions of success:

- It is the favourable outcome of an action.
- It is growth, development, improvement and getting better.
- It is achieving what you have set out to do.
- Getting good grades at school.
- Passing your driving test.
- Getting the job you wanted.
- You feel it when someone you love tells you that he/she loves you too.
- It is the pleasant and powerful feeling of achievement.
- You experience it when you win or earn a large sum of money.
- When you see your garden blooming.
- After meditating for ten minutes, without thoughts disturbing you.
- When you fix a broken instrument with your own hands.
- It is promotion at work.
- Shedding a few surplus pounds.
- Seeing your business prospering.
- Becoming famous.

It is all these things and many more.

You may enjoy it in the small daily events of life, and you can find it in great achievements. Some seek it in money and material possessions, and others seek it in inner peace and strength. Some seek it in both. What does it mean to you? Do you expect it? Do you believe you can attain it, and what do you plan to do in order to enjoy it?

Remember, success is not only something spectacular. It manifests also in the small things of daily life. You can enjoy it many times, every day.

You might desire to gain a large sum of money, become the owner of successful firm, become a successful and famous Actor, Singer or Writer, a great Inventor, Legislator, President or a Prime Minister. Your goal might be to succeed in inner work and meditation, gain psychic power, mind power or peace of mind and spiritual awakening. Some just desire a carefree life, health, love and happiness, and to have a good job with a good pay to enable them to live comfortably. Whatever your goal is, there are some inner qualities and powers, which are required for its achievement:

- The ability to decide exactly what you want to achieve
- A strong desire
- Visualization
- Concentration
- Willpower
- Self-discipline
- Persistence

Focus your mind on your desire, add the necessary mental and emotional ingredients, and voila. You manifested your desire.

4

HOW TO IMPROVE YOURSELF

Nowadays, the terms self-improvement, self-growth and self-help have become popular. It seems that people are turning inside to find the solution to their problems. They seek knowledge, techniques, workshops, lectures and teachers who can show them the way. People begin to understand that self-improvement and self-growth improve the quality of life.

The subconscious mind is one of the major keys to self-improvement and self-growth. By changing the contents of the subconscious mind you change your habits, behaviour and attitudes. This is brought about through visualization, affirmations, meditation and by analyzing behavior and habits.

The process of inner change requires inner work. It is not enough to read articles and books. You also have to practice what you read, and this requires time and effort. There is no such thing as instant self-improvement. Inner changes take some time, and there must be motivation, desire, ambition, perseverance and dedication. Outer and inner resistance and opposition must be taken into account too. When you start a self-improvement programme, it is common to encounter inner resistance that comes from your old habits and from your subconscious mind, and also resistance and opposition from the people around you.

The desire to change, build new habits and improve must be strong enough to resist any laziness, desire to give up and the ridicule or opposition from family, friends or colleagues.

Some instructions for self-improvement and growth technique are given below:

1. Look around you and watch how people behave in various circumstances. Watch the people you meet at home, work, at the supermarket, on the bus, train and on the street. Watch and learn also from people interviewed on TV, and also from movies.
2. Watch how people talk, walk and react, and how they are consequently, treated by others.
3. Pay attention to the way people use their voice and how they react to others' voices. Watch how you feel and act when people shout or speak softly. Watch what happens when people get angry, restless and upset and what happens if they are calm and relaxed.
4. If you do not like what you see, analyze what and why you do not like it, and then analyze your own behavior to find out whether you behave in the same way. Be honest and impartial in your analysis.
5. If you discover that you manifest some of these undesirable traits of character and behaviour, affirm to yourself often, that every time you manifest these traits or behaviour, you are going to be conscious and aware of them, and do your best to avoid them.
6. Play in your mind a mental scene of how you would like to behave. Repeat it several times a day, every day.
7. When you detect in someone a sort of behaviour or character traits you like and desire to possess, try

to act in a similar way. Here too, visualize several times each day a scene, where you act and behave in that different way.

8. You can also decide to change some habit and behaviour patterns and develop new ones, because you believe they are necessary and beneficial, even without seeing them in others first.
9. Think and visualize over and again in your mind how you would like to act and behave. Constantly remind yourself of the changes you desire to make, and strive to act according to them. Every time that you find yourself acting according to your old habit, remember your decision to change and improve, and act accordingly.
10. Do not be disappointed or frustrated if you do not attain fast results. It does not matter how many times you fail or forget to behave as you desired. Persevere with your efforts and never give up, and you will begin to see how you and your life change.

A SIMPLE TECHNIQUE FOR SELF-IMPROVEMENT

Self-improvement can turn into an enjoyable, rewarding and empowering activity. Look at the people around you and watch how they behave. If you find a trait of character or a certain behaviour, which you do not like, examine yourself closely and as impartially as possible, and find out whether you act or behave in the same way. If you do, then think and visualize how you would like to behave in a similar situation. Then, whenever you have the time, perform mental rehearsals of the new behaviour. Visualize yourself in the same situation, but acting in the way you want to behave.

Think often about the importance and advantages of a changed and more positive behaviour. Tell yourself again and again that you will remember to act differently the next time you are in a situation or circumstances that trigger the behaviour patterns that you want to change.

At the first attempts you will probably forget to act as desired, but keep visualizing and thinking about the new behaviour patterns, and you will see how you gradually change.

Whenever you see people acting in a way that brings them positive results, analyze what they are doing, their body language and the way they are talking and acting, and try to act and behave the same. If you keep doing so, you will soon start to see changes in yourself and in your life.

The advantage of this technique is that you can use it everywhere, anytime, without any prior preparations. Furthermore, this can turn in to a pleasurable game. You can use this technique while waiting for someone or something, while sitting on a bench in a park or while travelling in a bus or train. You can use your time more advantageously, instead of just letting the time pass by.

Here is an example of this self-improvement technique: You see one of your co-workers acting angrily. You watch his body language and the tone of his voice and see how people avoid him because of that. Now, look into yourself with an unbiased eye, and find out if you are guilty of the same kind of behaviour. If you are not, that's okay, but if you are, think about the consequences of this behaviour and the advantages of acting differently. Think how a calm and happy attitude can change your life and how people would treat you.The next step is to visualize yourself in circumstances that trigger the kind of behaviour you wish to avoid, and to see yourself acting in a new and positive manner. Rehearse in your mind, in detail, how you would like to act, so that when you encounter this situation, your subconscious mind will guide you to act as you visualized. Mentally rehearsing the new behaviour will remind you to act so in real life, and will also motivate and direct you to act accordingly.

Here is another example. You enter a shop and ask the saleswoman some questions. She is patient, calm and answers all of your questions politely and with a smile. Her behaviour causes you to feel good and to like her, which may consequently make you to desire to buy something from her.

Analyze the behaviour of the saleswoman, and see what you can do to emulate her. Tell yourself over and over again that you too, are going to behave politely and patiently. Visualize yourself in various situations that usually make you angry and impatient, and ask yourself why you behave in that way. Then start visualizing yourself acting and talking in a calm, polite and patient manner in your day-to-day life.It is important to understand that thinking and visualizing just once is not enough. You need to do so over and over again every day, even several times a day, until you see results.

The above examples are only meant to illustrate how to make use of this self-improvement technique. Maintain an open mind, open your eyes, desire to improve yourself, learn from others, affirm and visualize, and your life will begin to change.

Do you sometimes hear yourself or other people say: "I have tried positive thinking, and I have repeated affirmations, I have meditated and yet nothing happened"? The fact is that few people use self-improvement or positive thinking techniques correctly, and fewer still do so earnestly and whole-heartedly. You may start enthusiastically making affirmations for a few days, waiting for miracles, yet nothing spectacular happens. This makes you lose your enthusiasm and any confidence you had, and you disappointedly stop affirming.

You may start visualizing something you want to accomplish or get, but when after a few days the object of your desire does not drop on your head from the sky, you lose your faith and stop visualizing.

Maybe you have begun to meditate, but after a week or two saw no bright lights, neither experienced any altered state of consciousness. This made you conclude that meditation is just a waste of time.

Self-improvement and positive thinking methods work and bring results, but only if they are used correctly. You cannot build a building, a bridge or an airplane, without the proper knowledge, training and preparation, and following instructions and rules. Self-improvement and positive thinking methods should be approached in the same manner. You need to know how to use these techniques.

It is not enough to say for a few moments, "I am achieving my goal, I am happy, I have money", and then revert to negative thinking and worrying. There is no magic in repeating a few words for a few moments.

How can you expect to accomplish anything by visualizing, and at the same time worrying and having doubts about your ability to get what you are visualizing? How can you get any positive results if you sit for meditation, but instead of meditating you think about all kinds of irrelevant matters?

Success comes only if you fully and whole-heartedly desire what you are affirming or visualizing and concentrate on the task. In order to see results you have to show interest and earnestness and do your best. Your inner vision should be strong enough to propel you forward, no matter how negative your current situation is, and despite any failures you may experience.

If you think, visualize, affirm or meditate for a few minutes, and then for the rest of the day think negatively, you neutralize or destroy all your positive thoughts, mental images and affirmations.

Self-improvement techniques and positive thinking work and bring results, if you are determined to succeed, follow the instructions correctly, persevere and do not let lack of faith, laziness and procrastination stand in your way. You need to give these methods time to work.

If you practice them as an unpleasant task, with no attention and concentration, how do you expect them to work? Be willing to devote time, energy and effort, where and when necessary. Success in self-improvement and positive thinking methods requires that you become involved, motivated and be willing to give them enough time to bring results.

Sometimes things happen in such a way that you could label them as miracles, but most of the time things happen in a more natural and gradual way. Inner changes will start to manifest, and will lead to outer change. Doors will open, people will help, circumstances and situations will change, and new constructive ideas will come up, all of which will bring the desired changes and improvements.

INNER CHANGES BRING OUTER CHANGES

The quality of your life depends to a large extent on the quality of your inner emotional and mental life. If you are lazy, worry too much and afraid to try new things, you stick to the same spot. If you are not afraid to change your thinking, your life will soon change accordingly. Your habitual thoughts, and the content of your subconscious mind determine your behaviour and the way you act in the world.

When you change the way you feel and think, you ultimately change your inner vision, actions and behavior. This causes your outer life to change accordingly.

Let's now see a few examples!

If you are the worrying type, you are probably afraid of changes, and prefer to stick to the same kind of life you well know. You see other people who attain success, and though you wish you were successful too, you do nothing about it. In your mind you see yourself living exactly as you are living now, and find it hard to imagine different circumstances. It may never occur to you that you can visualize a different reality.

In this case your way of thinking limits you. You constantly see in your mind's eye the same daily reality, and consequently your conscious and subconscious minds stay programmed to experience and attract the same kind of reality.

Suppose you come to understand and realize that your outer reality is shaped to a great extent by your inner world. This realization will cause you to aspire to a better life. You will start to envision the kind of life you want to live. If you keep thinking and visualizing a different and better kind of life, soon these thoughts will sink into your subconscious mind and motivate, inspire and energize you to take action.

The new thoughts will cause new expectations, and change the way you view the outer world. The inner changes in you will gradually affect your outer life. Your behaviour, and the way you act will change. You will have more energy, ambition and inner strength. You will get over your fear of change, and be ready to take action to change and improve your life, in accordance with the changes inside you.

SELF-ACCEPTANCE

We hear so much about self-acceptance from people, who study or teach personal growth methods. What is self-acceptance? Does it mean accepting your weaknesses or negative habits and doing nothing about them? Does this mean accepting your behaviour, attitude and life style, and doing nothing to change and improve? This can be an easy way to give in to laziness, and to having good excuses for leaving everything as it is. This kind of self-acceptance might make you feel a little better and alleviate feelings of guilt, but it does not contribute to real progress and improvement.

The term self-acceptance seems not to be well explained and well understood. Accepting yourself as you are is only the first step. It helps you realize your good and not so good qualities, and can alleviate lack of self-esteem, lack of satisfaction and the sense of unhappiness.

Self-acceptance does not mean that you accept what you are and do nothing to change and improve. It does not mean accepting your fate and life as it is. Becoming aware and acknowledging your behaviour, habits and your personality, and not being afraid to look at yourself as you are, is the first step to self-acceptance.

When you accept yourself as you are, you put yourself in a better position to begin improving yourself. It is not an excuse for saying, "This is what I am. I accept myself as I am. I accept my character, my failings and my fate, and this how it is. I can do nothing about it." Knowing yourself affords you the possibility to see what you can do to improve yourself and your life.

Improvement requires that you understand and acknowledge your character and habits, stop comparing yourself and your achievements to others, and acknowledging your skills or the lack of them. This will bring some sort of inner peace, lightness and happiness, like getting rid if a burden. This is the first step to self-acceptance. Acknowledging your good and bad habits and traits of character can alleviate feelings of dissatisfaction, anger, resentment or unhappiness, but it is not an excuse for staying as you are, it is only the first step.

OVERCOMING ANXIETY

Anxiety in various forms and degrees seems to be a wide-spread problem, affecting people of all ages and in every country. If you are prone to anxiety, you have two options:

(a) Give in, and live with it.

(b) Learn to overcome it.

By giving in, you will continue to suffer and feel unhappy, stressed and anxious. It is far better to learn to overcome anxiety, or at least weaken its grip over you.

Anxiety wastes your time and energy and weakens you, both mentally and physically. You help no one, and solve no problem by being anxious. Our planet will go on revolving, even if you stop worrying and being anxious. Always know you have a choice—to give in to anxiety, or to try to overcome anxiety, at least partially.

Here are some tips for overcoming anxiety, or at least alleviating it:

1. Lack of control over your thoughts, strengthens your anxiety. As negative thoughts get stronger, your anxiety gets stronger too. You need to learn to control your thoughts.
2. Feelings and emotions fuel and strengthen anxiety. You need to develop some self-discipline, and learn to have control over your feelings. You also need to develop some degree of emotional detachment.

3. When you go to bed at night, and first thing when you wake up in the morning, think about the good things that are happening to you. There are always some good things happening, even if small and insignificant.
4. Start the day with several minutes of positive affirmations. Tell yourself how would like your day to be. Use positive, cheering and motivating words.
5. Be busy and do something, since activity keeps your mind off your anxiety. When you wake up in the morning, start doing something right away, and keep busy all day. Cleaning the house, washing the dishes or working in your garden, reading, studying, meditating, or exercising your body can help you keep your mind away from anxiety.
6. Set a goal and work everyday to achieve it. This action will direct your thoughts and feelings away from worries and anxieties, toward something more positive and constructive.
7. Talk about your anxieties to someone you trust. Talking about your anxieties and feelings can alleviate them, and put them in the right proportions, provided you talk objectively, and with a real desire to get rid of your anxiety, or at least reduce its intensity.
8. Exercising your body and staying fit, is a good way to keep fears and anxieties away. You can walk, swim, do yoga, aerobics, or any other sport.
9. Find reasons to laugh. This will bring light and happiness into your life, and drive anxiety away. Watch comedies on TV, be with happy and amusing friends, or read something that makes you laugh.
10. Use positive words in your conversation and in your inner talk.

11. Affirm and visualize positive situations and events. Visualize a happy and positive solution to your problems.
12. If watching the news fills you with anxiety—turn off the TV! Limit the time you watch the news, and don't watch anything that might upset you, before you go to bed.

MANAGE YOUR ANGER

Anger comes out as a response to feelings of dissatisfaction, frustration and unhappiness, which usually arise when we dislike a person, an object or a situation. It usually appears when we are unable to fulfil our wishes and desires, or when we are forced to do something we dislike doing or we would better avoid. In such situations, the mind reacts by feeling unhappy and stressed, which leads to anger.

Day-to-day life confronts us with many situations, which can produce anger. Your partner, children or friends might not do what you expect them to do. You might run out of coffee for your morning coffee. You might arrive late to the station and find that the bus or train has already left. You might need to meet someone you don't like, or someone might criticize you. All these situations, and many similar ones, can cause anger. The question is, do we have to react automatically or can we change our reactions and avoid anger?

Anger is a most negative reaction, and should be avoided as much as possible, if you wish to progress on the path of self-improvement. You cannot avoid all the situations that cause anger, however, with some training you can learn to control and change your reactions and attitude. You can teach yourself not to get angry.

You need to be aware of the situations that could lead to anger, and be alert enough when you experience them.

Do you want to react automatically, like a robot, or do you want to act consciously and control your reactions? You can overcome anger, but this requires some inner work.

1. When you feel uncomfortable and unhappy, stop what you are doing and visualize some pleasant mental scene from the past. Think of something that made you happy.
2. When you feel that you are getting angry, breathe deeply about 5 deep times. This will delay the anger and calm you down.
3. Count slowly from one to ten. This will delay your angry reaction and weaken it.
4. During your spare time, think about what anger leads to, and how worthwhile it is to avoid it.
5. Drink some water. This has a calming effect on the body.
6. Learn to develop some patience. Take simple tasks and do them slowly. This will develop patience.
7. One of the best remedies to anger is *detachment*. When you are emotionally and mentally detached, you cannot get angry.
8. The best way to avoid anger is to develop the habit of *peace of mind*. This of course needs some training and time, but is most worthwhile. Positive thinking, detachment, concentration and meditation, all lead to peace of mind.

MANAGE YOUR STRESS

Stress consumes your time and energy and weakens your immune system. It causes restlessness, unhappiness, impatience and anger. It can harm your life, ambitions, relationships and health. There is no doubt that it would be much better to live without it.

There are various methods to reduce, control and manage stress. Some stress management techniques may suit some people, and other techniques may suit other people.

In my opinion, one of the best methods for stress management is meditation. It exerts a calming effect on the body, nerves and blood pressure, reduces restlessness, and brings peace of mind, detachment and equanimity. To experience the benefits of meditation one needs to meditate everyday, but the problem is that not everyone has the discipline, will and desire to meditate, even when realizing the benefits of meditation.

It is not always possible to control or eliminate the reasons of stress, but it is possible to act and behave in certain ways that could reduce or alleviate it. You cannot always control the conditions of your life and circumstances, but you can learn to choose not to be internally influenced by them too much.

The following tips for stress management serve as first aid against stress. They will not prevent it altogether, but they can reduce or alleviate it.

Tips for Stress Management

- When you feel stress is building up within you, if possible, stop what you are doing and take a short walk.
- When stressed, drink some water or juice.
- When under stress, take a few slow deep breaths.
- Eat some food you like, because food can calm down restlessness and nervousness.
- Listen to your favorite music.
- Do something that you like doing.
- Watch a funny movie.
- Repeat affirmations to calm you down, such as:

- My mind is getting calm.
- I am relaxed and happy.
- I can meet any situation with calmness and inner strength.
- Everything is going to turn out great.
- I feel how my body, feelings and mind are getting calmer.

- Think, and persuade yourself about the futility of stress, and how much it is better to live without it.
- Exercise your inner freedom, and do not to let other people thoughts, opinions, words and actions affect you.
- Engage in sports or physical activity.

You can manage stress if you put your mind to it. It requires some effort and time on your part, but the rewards are great. Follow the tips, but also remember that the more peaceful your mind becomes, the less stress you experience. The more inner peace you possess, the less anxiety, stress and fear you experience.

PRINCIPLE OF MUTUALITY

The Principle of Mutuality is a universal principle that says that every interaction we have with another is based on mutual agreement. By this, we mean that the interaction must be fair and beneficial to both parties. Only in this way can the interaction become truly meaningful and healthy. The acceptance of this principle is implied in every relationship. Problems arise when this principle is violated. Violation can be at the conscious level or the unconscious level.

Taking What is not Given

At the conscious level, we violate this principle each time we consciously intent and act to take from others what is not given. This includes the taking of intangible as well as tangible things. Tangible things are things like properties, belongings, money and even this body. Intangiblesare things like life, rights, space, time, self-esteem, choices, values and trust. Avoiding taking tangible things from others without their explicit permissions is easier as it requires coarser awareness. Avoiding taking intangible things from others, on the other hand, requires more awareness and attention on our part.

We also often violates the principle of mutuality in an unconscious way. By this I mean that we are not fully aware of having violated this principle. Perhaps we did not have the conscious intention to take what is not given to us but due to our lack of self-awareness, we nevertheless violated it. To prevent this unconscious violation requires a much higher level of self-awareness from us. It requires courageous introspection and the examination of our habitual mental tendencies. Only then can we eliminate this unintentional violation of the principle of mutuality.

Giving Away our Power

Another source of problems with this principle is when we ourselves give away our power to the other party. Most often, we do this unconsciously and unintentionally. When we do not know how to be assertive with our rights, we dis-empower ourselves. When we do not even know our own rights, we do not know what we have given away. Thus, knowing our rights and being assertive are two essential elements to empowering ourselves. Knowledge is required for the former and courage for the latter.

Two to Tango?

The principle of mutuality is a spiritual principle that

governs relationships. When adhered to, it can bring forth spiritually fulfilling encounters and outcomes for everyone in the relationships. This is the ideal spiritual relationship. It is a win-win and is conducive to growth and personal transformation.

Although every relationship involves two or more parties, it does not mean that if the other party chooses to violate this principle, you on your own cannot adhere to it. In fact, irregardless of whether the other party is aware of or adhere to this principle of mutuality or not, you can continue to live in accordance with it.

The Right Attitude

All it needs to succeed with this principle is to have the right attitude. What is the right attitude? When interacting with another, ask yourself "How can I make this interaction beneficial, meaningful and fulfilling to all concerned?"

This approach working out very well for general practitioner. This approach is suitable for all types of interactions, including personal, social and business, and strongly encourage that you give it a try. You would be amazed at the results.

Mutuality in Relationships

There is a universal rule or principle that, if properly practiced and adhered to in every layer of societies, will bring about peace, prosperity and justice for all. This principle is called the principle of mutuality. Elsewhere in the scriptures, it is also known as the Golden Rule or "do unto others as you would want others to do unto you".

The principle of mutuality is based on the recognition that life is precious to all living beings and that every being has the equal right to life, liberty and self-expression, provided that in expressing yourself you do not trample on another being's similar rights. For this principle to work effectively, there is a need for openness, honesty and courage, and the realization that we are all subjected to the universal law of cause and effect. You reap what you sow.

In practical terms, what this means is that you have the same universal rights as everyone else. You do not have more rights than another. Neither do you have less rights than others. This is irregardless of whether you are rich or poor; a Christian, Muslim, Hindu, Buddhist or Jew; a European, Asian, African or Aborigine; a male or female; or whether you are smarter or dumber than others. Likewise, in corporations and governments, you have these same rights to demand for equal justice, regardless of whether you are the governed or the governor.

In our relationships with others, this principle is particularly important in bringing about an equal and enriching partnership. When adhered to, it brings about respect for each other, fair play and sharing of roles and responsibilities. It encourages personal and mutual growth, as well as spiritual development. However, putting this principle into practice is not easy as it requires a high degree of self-awareness, a non-judgmental attitude and especially the taming of the ego.

The ego has this attitude that "I am more important than you". Thus we often see how it tries to manipulate every relationship to its own advantage at the expense of others. In a position of power, it will abuse its power. We see this in government and institutional leaders as well as in homes and families. We see this in teacher-student relationships as well. Even among friends, we need to be aware of this dynamics.

If I ask you to examine your own key relationships, such as husband-wife, parent-child, and employer-employee relationships, are you able to honestly say that these relationships are equal and fair for all concern, or are they heavily leaning to one side? One simple way to know whether our relationship is balanced is to see how happy the two persons in the relationship are. If it is well balanced, then both are equally happy. If either one is unhappy or both are, then an unequal dynamic exists. The more it diverts from the center, the more unhealthy the relationship is, and the more important it is for you to do something about it. Leaving such one-sided relationships in status quo only serves to perpetuate this inequality in your relationships as well as in society. In addition, inaction on your part breeds contempt for yourself and squashes your personal and spiritual growth.

PRINCIPLE OF ACCOUNTABILITY

We are responsible for every thought, word and deed of ours. The ancient masters said we are the owner of our deeds and we are the result of them.

Once we understand the concept of *as we sow, so we reap,* we will understand that whatever we get out of our lives is a result of what we have planted in our mind. Our past mental imprints determine our present situation in life, and the mental imprints that we plant now will determine our future situation.

The ancient sages liken this to planting a garden. If we want a beautiful garden, we will have to selectively plant beautiful plants. What is equally important is that we must constantly pull out the weeds. Without doing that, our garden will be overrun by weeds, obscuring the beautiful plants. Likewise, to plant for a beautiful life, we must select only the mental imprints that we want, and constantly weed out the unuseful or harmful mental imprints. This, of course, requires constant mindfulness.

We need to continuously guard what goes pass our conscious mind into our subconscious mind.

What this means is that we are fully responsible and accountable for our lives. We cannot blame anyone or anything for what is happening in our lives. Unfortunately, we often have this unhealthy tendency to blame someone or something. We unconsciously look for someone to blame when things go wrong in our lives rather than accept that we reaped what we sow.

Funnily, though, when good things come into our lives, we somehow believe we deserve them. We rarely look outside for someone to praise. If we would blame others for the bad things, why do we not praise others for the good things in our lives?

Blaming others is our way of avoiding taking responsibility for our lives. As long as we do that, we will never be the master of our lives. To counter this unhealthy tendency, we should instead cultivate a sense of gratitude towards all that we received.

Here are two methods you can use to cultivate a sense of gratitude:

1. *The Gratitude Book.* At the end of each day, review your day and count your blessings. Write these down in a little note book. You may call this note book your Gratitude Book. By doing this consistently, you'll be retraining your mind to focus on the positive aspects of your life. Why is this important? Because like attracts like. The more you focus on the positive in life, the more positive things will come your way.
2. *Altruistic Joy.* Altruistic joy is a concept borrowed from the Buddhists. It means rejoicing at other people's good fortune. This practice counters our tendency to be envious of another person's success. Each time we rejoice at other's success, we are

basically planting joyful imprints in our mind, thereby sowing seeds of joy for our own future.

RESOLVE CONFLICTS IN YOUR LIFE

Conflicts are bound to arise in our relationships from time to time. Very often, conflicts arise from simple mis-communication. At other times, conflicts are due to clashes of personalities.

Each of us deals with conflicts differently. There are at least 5 ways in which we can deal with conflicts, but not all of them lead to desirable outcomes. Can you identify which of these ways you predominantly use to resolve conflicts in your life?

1. *Avoidance.* "It's not a big problem. Why rock the boat?"
2. *Accommodation.* "I'm willing to give up a lot to avoid conflicts."
3. *Aggression.* "I intend to win this conflict."
4. *Compromise.* "I'll give in a little if you're also giving in a little."
5. *Problem Solving.* "If we discuss this honestly and openly, everyone can win."

Not all of these styles are beneficial in the long run. The first three may avoid or delay conflicts, or kick the can down the road a little, but conflicts are not truly resolved. They may in fact fester and get worse later.

If you are using method 1 and 2, you may not be assertive enough and may in fact be treated like a doormat by others. If you prefer method 3, you may actually worsen the conflicts more often than not. Method 4 gives a satisfactory outcome but the best and most matured method is 5.

SIMPLIFY YOUR LIFE

The modern lifestyle is a stressful lifestyle. It is based on the belief that more is better—more things to do, more things accomplished, more gains, more activities, more sense stimulation. Thus the need to have more money and more possessions. However, such a life is not necessarily more fulfilling. In fact, it often leads to a more stressful life, more sickness and more frustrations. Great rewards await those who can simplify their lives. A simple life can be more fulfilling, more peaceful and more beneficial to you. It can be more conducive to a happier and healthier life, and it can improve your relationships tremendously. Here are some steps to simplify your life:

1. Prioritize

The first thing to do is to spend some time to decide what is truly important to you. Is it your health, time with loved ones or service to community? It might interest you to know that people in their death beds do not worry about how much money or properties they have accumulated. Rather, they are concern about the quality of the relationships they have, and they are particularly worried about any unfinished business or unresolved conflicts with their loved ones. Rather than repairing damaged relationships when we are dying, is it not wiser to cultivate quality relationships while we are still healthy and alive?

2. Slow-Down

Do not measure your life by the number of tasks you do each day. Many people squeeze as many tasks as they can into their day, thinking that the more they do, the more they achieve. In doing so, they are able to accomplish more tasks but at the expense of truly living and enjoying the tasks they do. They sacrifice quality for the number. The way to truly live is to slow down and enjoy each moment and task that you do. Make each task meaningful. Be present in the moment instead of rushing through the task. When you have worked out your priorities, you will be able to know what is important and what is not, and you can then reduce the unnecessary tasks, leaving you with more time for the more important tasks.

3. Discard the Unnecessary

Take time to unclutter your life. Begin by uncluttering your possessions. Look at your table. Check out the storerooms. Are there anything there that you can discard? Are you hoarding too many things in your life? The habit of hoarding is a sign of insecurity, a manifestation of fear. The more things you need to feel safe indicates the more fear in you. Material possessiveness is just one sign of this insecurity. Look within your mind and you will probably see that there are many more sense of insecurity in your thoughts. Learn to let go of those fear too. The more you let go, the lighter you will feel, and paradoxically the less you fear. Remember that there are many people who have been able to live with far less than what you have. Note also that the more you feed this hoarding habit, the stronger it gets and the more insecure you will feel.

4. Reduce Information Overload

Our modern life is bombarded by information from all directions. We are reachable every minute with our mobile phones, and we are constantly connected to news via the internet, emails, social networks and the traditional newspapers, televisions and radios. If we want to find some peace of mind, we need to reduce all these bombardments. We need to be able to switch off our phones, computers, televisions and radios, and reward ourselves with some time free from all these intrusions. We need to spend some quiet and uninterrupted time with ourselves and our loved ones.

5. Learn Gratitude

Rather than cultivating a habit of feeding our wants and needs, which is like a bottomless black-hole that can never be filled, it is more fruitful to cultivate a habit of reducing our wants and needs. Learn instead to be grateful for whatever we have. We can be grateful for all the things that went right in our life, such as the party we planned for our child's birthday, a wonderful weekend trip with the family or simply spending a restful evening with our loved ones. Try it and you will find that it is easy to fall in love with the simple life.

FIND PEACE OF MIND

The world we live in today is in chaos. Greed and hatred are seen manifesting everywhere. People are living in fear, feeling a great sense of insecurity and frustration. Government and financial systems are falling apart. Nothing seems to be working. In a world where chaos seems to reign, is there any hope of finding peace? Here are a few tips to reclaim the peace and sense of safety missing in your life today.

1. Look Within

Instead of trying to fix things outside, let us begin by fixing what is wrong inside—within ourselves. Examine our values, beliefs and the principles we uphold. Take a good and honest look at our motivations. Are our actions motivated by fear or by love? We are now experiencing the effects of actions that were motivated by greed (financial collapse) and hatred (terrorism). We should know by now that if our motivation is not pure, the end result cannot be good, even if it may look good in the short term.

2. Eliminate Fear and Selfishness

The more we feed fear, the stronger fear grows. We need to recognize and acknowledge the fear within us, and face our fear. Only when we do that can we learn to overcome our own fear. It is possible to live a life without fear. Indeed, that is what ultimately freedom means—the freedom from fear.

Again, when we look at the world outside, we are seeing repressive regimes that promote fear and exploit their people are now having to deal with the backlash of such repressions. Fear cannot sustain itself. Eventually, it will fail.

The same is true for us as well. If we let fear becomes the motivating force in our life—in our behaviors and actions—it will eventually fail us too. If we look closely, we will realize that selfishness is a form of fear. Therefore, we need to eliminate selfishness.

3. Seek Peace within You

Peace is our birthright. It is our true nature, our essence. If we look within and eliminate fear, we will find peace within us. It has been there all the time. Only our fear and selfishness have blinded us and obscure our sight.

If you have been living fearfully all your life, it can be difficult to believe that peace is within you. Yet, you must have faith that this is true. Only then will you begin to seek it within. Once again, we can look at the world outside to learn that all who seek peace outside have not found it. Only those who seek peace within have found it. Ask the sages and the saints. They will tell you this simple truth.

Put these three simple tips into practice in your life and you will reap the benefits.

YOUR UNIVERSE BEGINS IN YOUR MIND

Our lives and the circumstances we live in are largely the result of our own thoughts and beliefs. The sum total of our thoughts, if they are positive, will result in a positive life for us. The converse is just as true. If we think negatively most of the time, we tend to attract negative circumstances into our life. This great truth is known to all mystics and ancient sages. They may have said it in different ways but they all point to the same thing.

The Buddhists know this as the Law of Kamma. Jesus said, "You reap what you sow." If you plant an apple seed, you get an apple tree. The seed is your thought imprint. The apple tree is what is manifested in your physical world. The ancient Egyptians called this phenomenon *as within, so without*. What they mean is that our outer physical world and circumstances are merely reflections of our inner mental realities.

Our thoughts are energetic waves and they are subjected to the Law of Sympathetic Resonance. According to this law, when an object with a specific frequency vibrates and is brought near another object with similar frequency, it will cause the second object to vibrate as well.

The classic example for this is that of a singer with a high-pitched voice breaking a glass. In science classes, this same principle is demonstrated by bringing a vibrating tuning fork to another tuning fork with similar frequency. The second tuning fork will start to vibrate on its own.In modern time, this universal principle is called the Universal Law of Attraction.

It is important to note that the second object can only vibrate if it is of similar frequency to the first object.

What this means is that *like attracts like.* The same principle applies to our thoughts and beliefs. The more good thoughts we have, the better our lives will be. The more positive thoughts we have the more positive circumstances we encounter in our lives. The same is true with the negative.

Another important principle to remember is that *our mind cannot differentiate good from bad.* More accurately, our subconscious mind cannot differentiate the good from the bad. This is because our subconscious mind largely represents our mind in its natural state—a mind that is pure and non-judgemental. Thus our conscious mind gets the important task of being the gatekeeper—guarding the thoughts that get into our subconscious mind. If you've ever tried to guard the thoughts that get into your subconscious mind, then you'll know what a formidable task this is. The more mindful or aware you are, the easier it is to guard what goes through your mind. We will deal with this mindfulness or self-awareness later.

Start applying these principles in your life by doing these:

(a). Guard every thought carefully. Be a conscious gatekeeper to your subconscious mind. Remember that whatever you think about, especially when combined with the emotions of desire or fear, you will attract into your life. So make sure you attract what you want for your life by constantly thinking only about what you truly want.

(b). Feed your mind constantly with new information, images and ideas of the person you want to be and the life you want to live. By creating this inner attitude of your mind, you change the outer aspects of your reality.

Do these two exercises daily for one week and see the positive transformation that comes into your life.

CHANGE YOUR BELIEFS AND CHANGE YOUR LIFE

Our mind is to our body what the software is to the computer. It controls the body. Whatever words and deeds that come out through your mouth or your body must first be conceived in your mind. Our belief system is comparable to the computer's operating system (OS). It determines how we respond or react to the external world and circumstances, and what we attract into our life.

If you look carefully at yourself, you'll realise that how you respond to a certain situation is largely dependant on your core beliefs. If you believe that the world out there is a dog-eat-dog world, you'll respond in a certain way. You'll put on your guard when you deal with people around you, with a greater degree of mistrust and apprehension. This is a common mindset in the business world.

Contrast that with your mindset when you're in a sacred place, for example in a church or a temple. Your responses toward people in such places are entirely different from your usual dealing with your business associates. Even your words become softer and gentler. Your entire mannerism changes.

So how we respond to the external world depends on our core beliefs.

Another fact to remember, and this is important if we want to change our life, is that our core beliefs also determine what we attract into our life. This is consistent with the Universal Law of Attraction that says like attracts like. This is because our belief system is like our computer's operating system. If your computer is running a Windows OS, your mind will only be attracted to softwares and programmes that is compatible with the Windows environment. It automatically overlooks programmes for Macs and Linux because you know you cannot run those programmes in your PC. Thus our belief system may limit our possibilities in life.

Likewise, if you believe in scarcity, you'll attract circumstances into your life that is consistent with that belief and so you'll find yourself in constant struggle to accumulate the wealth you want. Note that what you believe need not be what you want.

5

POWER OF CONCENTRATION AND MEDITATION

Concentration and Meditation are the two primary tools that each of us use to explore our lives.

Concentration means with a centre; it is the act or process of concentrating, focusing; the process of becoming concentrated, or the state of being concentrated, concretized. The hallmark of concentration is localization or focus; concentration is the cause of separation as it creates form.

Concentration is the extreme of awareness where there is the choice of focusing attention in a localized way—it is awareness with a choice. An example of concentration is a wave within the ocean as the current step that your are focusing on as part of a greater journey.

Meditation is the extreme of seeing that is present when concentration is absent. In other words meditation is the non-localized form of Seeing; it is like stepping back to be able to see the big picture.

Meditation is the extreme of awareness that is there naturally when concentrated focus is relaxed—it is choiceless awareness. An example of Meditation is the mirror-like stillness of water that reflects the nature of things. Meditation is the formlessness in which form appears.

By itself Concentration is like standing on one leg; it is very difficult to walk in harmony with the current of being with only one leg.

By itself Meditation is like standing on one leg; it is very difficult to walk in harmony with the current of being with only one leg.

Perhaps the most interesting attribute of Concentration and Meditation is that they simultaneously can compliment or negate each other. The negation is seen in the fact that when you wish to see fine detail it is necessary that you concentrate and focus in such a myopic manner that it is not possible to see the whole picture, and, when you do wish to see the whole picture it is necessary that you step back whereby you can no longer see the fine detail. The complimentary relationship is also available such that when your concentrate it is possible to allow a relaxed meditative concentration in which you see the whole of whatever it is you have focused on, and, your meditations may have a concentrated focus as you *weigh* your choices in a particular situation.

Both Concentration and Meditation are processes; you use the one that is appropriate to the situation in the bigger process called life. The unfolding process is like a journey that you are taking by walking where you first stand on one foot and leg and then you shift things over to the other as you explore your way of living.

BODY AND MIND

The activities of your mind are generally what is called thinking and its substance is said to be thoughts. The activities of your body is feeling and its substance is said to be sensations. Obviously these two form One

Integrated Reality that mirrors the inter-relationship of Concentration and Meditation.

Your localized mind is the instrument that you use when you wish to focus and concentrate on a particular task or activity. And with steady concentration and focus your thoughts become clearer and more concretized as the process unfolds.

Your body is the instrument that you use to get in touch with your feelings. Feelings are very distinct, yet by nature they are not very easy to describe because the describing requires that you concentrate on your feelings and translate them into thoughts. And yet your feelings are much more reliable than your thoughts as guides along the journey of your life, because they have embedded within them that meditative quality that allows you to see the big picture of your journey.

In this light it is clear that just as you emphasize Concentration or Meditation depending on the situation; you also use the intelligence of your body or your mind as appropriate to the situation. And together they form the vehicle whereby you experience life.

Thus far you have seen that Concentration and Meditation and your Body and Mind are the primary instruments that you use in your life's journey. And you see that the one you use is the one that is determined by the situation.This is an objectification of these instruments and processes such that they can be clearly seen; in other words this description is Concentration. After reading this it is helpful to allow some time for the words to be assimilated such that they impact you on a deeper level. In other words it is helpful that you also embrace the meditative component of Seeing as you explore these tools. And, finally it must be noted that although there is kind of separation as these things are being described, the ultimate Truth is that there is no separation because these are not just tools of life—

together, they form the pillars on which your life is built. Thus these tools are not separate from each other. In fact each has some of the other in it, and together as your mind-body they are One Integrated Reality. The other attribute of each of these tools is that each is a living process.

The togetherness of these instruments is a kind of weaving that creates the fabric of your life. This is a communication process between the processes of Concentration and Meditation and your Body and Mind whereby you adjust to the changing circumstances of your life. This communication is clearly revealed in Breathing; Breath is Life.

In this light Breath is not a tool. Breathing is the central current of your Being. Breath is Life and Breathing is the mean between your body and mind as it is more subtle than your body and more gross than your mind. You will live for as long as you breathe and when you are no longer breathing, life as you know it will cease to exist.

You appear as a separate individual. And although the Ultimate Truth is that nothing is separate, this does not deny the fact that you are a localized, concentrated, Being. Thus one extreme of your Being is Concentration: this is akin to your respiration as inspiration; the other extreme of your Being is Meditation: this is akin to your respiration as expiration. Together these form respiration or re-spiriting.

In this way you see that Breath literally is Life, and that the place of communion between the extremes of the communication process of the instruments of your being is the space where the journey of your life unfolds harmoniously. It will always be a journey with its many ups and downs, yet when you understand the spirit and nature of it, then you live in the joy and wonder of the miracle of life itself—You are the Miracle of Life.

POWER OF CONCENTRATION

When our mind is focused, our energies are not dissipated on irrelevant activities or thoughts. This is why developing concentration is essential to anyone who aspires to take charge of his or her life. This skill is essential for every kind of success. Without it, our efforts get scattered, but with it, we can accomplish great things.

Concentration has many uses and benefits. It assists in studying and understanding faster, improves the memory, and helps in focusing on any task, job, activity or goal, and achieving it more easily and efficiently. It is also required for developing psychic powers, and is a powerful tool for the efficient use of creative visualization.

When this ability is developed, the mind obeys us more readily and does not engage in futile, negative thoughts or worries. We gain mental mastery and we experience true peace of mind.

This ability also plays an important role in meditation. Without it, the mind just jumps restlessly from one thought to another, not allowing us to meditate properly.

Do you now realize, why it is very important and worthwhile to develop and improve the ability to concentrate?

To develop this power you need to train and exercise it. Forget all your excuses about not having the time or being too busy. Do not say that the circumstances are not appropriate or that you cannot find a quiet place to exercise. With a little planning, desire and motivation you can always find the time to exercise each day, no matter how busy you are.

Developing Concentration

Thoughts claim our attention incessantly, and waste our

time and energy on unimportant and useless matters. They actually rule our life. We have become so used to this slavery, that we take it for granted, and have become unconscious of this habit, except on certain occasions.

While breathing, we do not need to pay attention to each inhalation and exhalation. We become conscious of the process of breathing, only when we have some difficulty with breathing, such as when our nose is clogged, due to a cold, or when we are in an unventilated room.

It is the same with thinking. We become conscious of the constant onslaught of our thoughts, and of our inability to calm them down, only when we need to concentrate, solve a problem or study. We are also acutely aware of them when we have worries or fears.

Look at the following familiar situation. You need to study something for your job or for an exam. You sit comfortably on the sofa with the book in your hands and start reading. After a while you feel hungry and go to the kitchen to eat something.

You return to read, and then hear you people talking outside. You listen to them for several moments and then bring your attention back to the book.

After a while you feel restless and switch on the radio to listen to some music. You continue to read for a little while, and then remember something that happened yesterday, and you start thinking about it.

When you look at your watch, you are amazed to find out that one complete hour has passed and you have hardly read anything.

This is what happens when one lacks concentration. Imagine what you could have accomplished, if you could control your attention and focus your mind! Work that requires physical strength, such as carrying heavy loads for example, develops physical strength. Yet, it is not as exercising daily to the gym in a systematic manner. It is the same with concentration. Reading, studying and trying to pay attention to what we do, develop some of this ability, but practising exercises diligently each day is something else, it is like training in a gym.

Inner Resistance to Developing Concentration

In order to develop this ability we have to train our minds. Most people think that concentration is a strenuous and tiring activity, and that it involves exertion and tension, which are difficult and unpleasant. This belief starts at an early age. Parents and teachers expect children to study, do their homework and get good grades. This brings up in the children a feeling of being coerced and forced to do something they don't like doing. When they are too often told that they are not concentrating good enough, they develop a loathing for concentration, and often for studying too. These become associated with coercion, lack of freedom, doing something they do not like to do, and which is against their will. When they grow up, it is no wonder that their powers of concentration are weak, and they have no desire to strain their minds. Though most people acknowledge the fact that good concentration is a great asset, yet most of them do nothing to strengthen it, because they don't know how, and because they lack the motivation.

Concentration can be fun, if approached in the right way. It should be practiced with joy, positive attitude, optimism, and understanding of its great possibilities.

Benefits of Developing Concentration

Sometimes you can find strong powers of concentration in yourself. When you really and earnestly want to excel in your studies, pass an important exam or solve a problem, this power becomes available to you. In such cases, it appears because of some need or desire, but developing it in a systematic way brings it under your control, and grants you the ability to use it intentionally, whenever you need it. To do so, you need to practice special exercises on a daily basis.

Here is what you can gain by developing this power:

- Control of your thoughts.
- The ability to focus your mind.
- Peace of mind.
- Freedom from futile and annoying thoughts.
- The ability to choose your thoughts.
- Better memory.
- Self-confidence.
- Inner strength.
- Willpower.
- Decisiveness.
- The ability to study and comprehend more quickly.
- Inner happiness.
- Enhanced capability to develop psychic abilities.
- More powerful and efficient use of creative visualization.
- Enhanced ability to meditate.

And much more..

CONCENTRATION EXERCISES

Sharpening the needle of concentration requires practice, as everything else in life. Do you go to the gym? If you do, how many times during the week and for how long? Do you study a foreign language? If you do, how much time do you devote to it? Developing concentration is not different; training is required. Even ten minutes a day of concentration exercises will do you good.

The mind does not like discipline and will resist your efforts to discipline it. It loves its freedom more than anything else, and will try to stand in your way to master it, in any way it can. It will cause you to forget to do the exercises, tempt you to postpone performing them or make you feel too lazy. It will find many tricks to stop and disturb you, but you can and must be stronger.

You will find below, some simple *concentration exercises* to perform. Always remember that the choice is yours, to be a slave to the mind and its whims, or to be its master. By practising mental exercises, it is possible to train the mind and master it, and put it in its proper place, as your servant, and not as your boss and master.

You are not the mind nor the thoughts that pass through it. Though it might be hard to accept this idea, the mind is not you, the real you, but only a tool that you use. It is an instrument, which has great value, but it has to be taught to obey you.

Most people believe that they are the mind, and erroneously believe that controlling the mind means holding themselves back and denying their freedom. They feel that controlling their mind is not natural, and that it is some sort of repression. These beliefs are not correct. The proof that we are not the mind comes with training. Accept the idea in theory, and in time, as your control over your thoughts grows, you will know it as a fact. In reality, you, the real you, is the one mastering the mind. It is not the mind mastering itself.

Find a place where you can be alone and undisturbed. You can sit crossed legged on the floor if you can, or on a chair. Sit with your spine erect. Take a few calm deep breaths and then relax your body. Direct the attention to your body, and relax each muscle and part of it.

Here are some exercises for you to practice. Sit down to practice for about 10 minutes, and after a few weeks of training, lengthen the time to 15 minutes.

Start with the first exercise, practising it daily, until you are able to do it without any distractions or forgetfulness, and without thinking about anything else, for at least three continuous minutes. Every time you get distracted, start again, until the 10 or 15 minutes pass away. You have to be honest with yourself, and proceed to the next one, only after you are convinced that you have practiced it correctly and with full concentration.

Put your whole attention into the exercises, and do not think about anything else. Be careful not to fall asleep, day-dream or think about other matters. The moment you find yourself thinking about something else, stop the exercise and start again. After you become proficient, lengthen the time, and if possible, include another session in the afternoon. Do not attempt too much at the beginning, and don't try to perform them all at once. Go slowly, without overdoing them or tensing your brain.

If you find it too difficult, or thoughts distract you and make you think about other matters, don't despair. Everyone encounters difficulties along the way. If you persevere and never give up, in spite of difficulties and disturbances, success will crown your efforts. Remember, even those with powerful concentration had to exercise their minds.

It does not matter if your concentration is weak now, it can be developed and strengthened like any other ability, through training and investing the necessary time, energy and earnestness.

In time, you will find out that you can concentrate anywhere, anytime, no matter where you are. You will be able to focus your mind, think and function under the most trying circumstances, while remaining calm, relaxed and collected. The reward is worth the effort a thousand fold.

Now to the exercises. Some of them may be familiar to you, and some may seem too easy to perform. Some were taken from various sources, and others were created by me.

For full benefit, it is advisable that you practice each exercise for one additional week, after you are convinced that you are practising it correctly and with full attention.

Exercises

1. Take a book and count the words in any one paragraph. Count them again to be sure that you have counted them correctly. Start with one paragraph and when it becomes easier, count the words in a whole page. Perform the counting mentally and only with your eyes, without pointing you finger at each word.

2. Count backwards in your mind, from one hundred to one.

3. Count in your mind from one hundred to one, skipping each three numbers, that is 100, 97, 94, etc.

4. Choose an inspiring word, or just a simple sound, and repeat it silently in your mind for five minutes. When your mind can concentrate more easily, try to reach ten minutes of uninterrupted concentration.

5. Take a fruit, an apple, orange, banana or any other fruit, and hold it in your hands. Examine the fruit from all its sides, while keeping your whole attention focused on it. Do not let yourself be carried away by irrelevant thoughts or associated thoughts that might arise, such as about the shop were you bought it, about how and where it was grown, its nutritive value, etc. Stay calm, while trying to ignore these thoughts and not be interested in

them. Just look at the fruit, focus your attention on it without thinking about anything else, and examine its shape, smell, taste and the sensation it gives when touching and holding it.

6. This is the same as exercise number 5, only that this time you visualize the fruit instead of looking at it. Start by looking at the fruit and examining it for about 2 minutes, just as in exercise number 5, and then do this one. Close your eyes, and try to see, smell, taste and touch the fruit in your imagination. Try to see a clear and well defined image. If the image becomes blurred, open your eyes, look at the fruit for a short while, and then close your eyes and continue the exercise. It might help if you imagine the fruit held in your hands, as in the previous exercise, or imagine it standing on a table.

7. Take a small simple object such as a spoon, a fork, or a glass. Concentrate on one of these objects. Watch the object from all sides without any verbalization, that is, with no words in your mind. Just watch the object without thinking with words about it.

8. After becoming proficient in the above exercises, you can come to this exercise. Draw a small geometrical figure, about three inches in size, such as a triangle, a rectangular or a circle, paint it with any colour you wish, and concentrate on it. You should see only the figure, nothing else. Only the figure exists for you now, with no unrelated thoughts or any distractions. Try not to think with words during the exercise. Watch the figure in front of you and that's it. Try not to strain your eyes.

9. The same as number 8, only this time visualize the figure with the eyes closed. As before, if you forget how the figure looks like, open your eyes for a few seconds and watch the figure and then close your eyes and continue with the exercise.

10. The same as above in number 9 but the eyes open.

11. Try for at least five minutes, to stay without thoughts. This exercise is to be attempted only after all the previous ones have been performed successfully. The previous exercises, if practiced correctly, will endow you with the ability to impose silence on your thoughts. In time it will become easier and easier.

The secret of success is constant practice. The more time you devote to the exercises the faster your success arrives. Go on gradually; ten minutes at the start and in time as you gain the ability to concentrate, give it more time. When you see that you are successful, you will begin to love the exercises, and in time they will become a habit. You will be able to concentrate your attention easily and effortlessly upon anything you want to concentrate on.

Are you jogging, exercising at the gym or studying a foreign language? How difficult it was in the start? How many times you wanted to quit? Yet, after a while you started to like what you were doing. It became a habit, needing no effort to perform. So it is with developing the power of concentration.

After some of time you will start to feel differently. It will be easier to concentrate. Your mind will be calm and relaxed, and you will radiate peace into your surroundings. Things, circumstances and events that used to agitate and anger you, will not influence your inner calmness. You will experience happiness, content and satisfaction, self-confidence and inner strength. You will be able to cope more easily and efficiently with the outer world.

You will feel a new form of consciousness growing in you, bringing you peace of mind. It may come every now and then for a brief moment, but in time it will grow and fill you completely. You will be able to make the mind work for you when you need its services, in a most efficient way. You will be able to silence it when its services are not needed.

The attitude to life and the reactions to events change after starting to practice concentration. It is some kind of automatic and gradual process. You come to know many things about the mind and how it functions, and you learn to deal with it efficiently.

DEVELOPING POWER OF ATTENTION

We all know that attention is a very desirable skill, but how many possess it? I don't need to tell you why it is important, and what are its uses and benefits. It is a must for every person who desires to succeed, whether on a minor or a major scale, whether in the material or spiritual world. In order to gain success you need to be able to focus your mind, and to calm down its restlessness and tendency to constantly shift from one subject to another.

Every act needs attention for its successful performance. Working, talking, conversing, studying and playing require attention. Even washing, cleaning the house or cooking require it, in order to be handled efficiently.

People are not born with the power of attention. It has to be developed. Its development and training starts from a very early age. We try to grab the attention of a baby by making strange noises. Later we focus the attention of the child by reading him/her stories. As the children grow up they are required to concentrate on whatever they study or read. All of these activities help to some extent to develop and focus the power of attention, but they are not enough.

There are times when the attention becomes very strong, though involuntarily, and without exercising real control over it. You have certainly experienced a few times a total blankness to the outside world, when you were absorbed in an interesting thriller or while reading a captivating book. This usually happens when we engage in activities that we enjoy and love.

For this ability to be useful, it should be under the control of your will. You have to be able to decide where and when to focus your mind. Real and effective power of attention should be under your control, and you should be able to exercise it whenever you need it.

Every day you are presented with plenty of opportunities to strengthen the power of your attention. Actually, every action can be turned into an exercise. Hold your mind on whatever you do, and try to concentrate without deviating to something else. It is true that special concentration exercises are necessary, but if you cannot find the time and place to perform them, you can turn the whole day into an enjoyable exercise. Focus on whatever you do, and in time your ability would increase.

In this way you will not only strengthen your attention and concentration, but everything you do will be done better, more efficiently, and even faster. In time, as your attention gets stronger, thoughts will lose their power to distract you, and you will find that you can absorb yourself in whatever you do. This will increase your efficiency, and make you enjoy whatever you do.

Here a few suggestions for developing and strengthening the power of attention:

– When reading a book, focus your eyes and mind on the words, and do not to think of anything not connected with what you are reading. Ignore outside noises and any irrelevant thoughts.

– Dress up, and at the same time put your whole attention on your movements.

- While having a shower, pay attention to every part of the body that you are soaping and washing.
- When you clean the house, mow the grass or cook, concentrate on each act and movement, without daydreaming or thinking about something else.
- While working, focus your mind on what you are doing, as if it is the only important thing in the world, even if you do not like your job.
- While working up, walking or engaging in any kind of physical activity, don't daydream or think on whatever enters your mind. Instead, focus your attention on what you are doing.
- While conversing, listen attentively to what people are saying.
- While eating, focus your mind or your food and on enjoying it.
- Always do one thing at a time.

You don't have to do all the above, all the time. Even a few minutes, now and then, will do wonders for you, and develop your powers of attention. Persevere, and you will gain a very useful ability, which will help you on many occasions in your life.

MEDITATION—GUIDANCE AND TIPS

Meditation is more than a method for relaxing the body, as some people think. It is a way for gaining freedom from incessant, nagging thoughts and worries, quieting the chatter of the mind, and attaining inner peace and happiness. In its higher levels, it leads to spiritual awakening and enlightenment.

Meditation plays an important role in various religions and spiritual traditions, and has always been practiced everywhere, from ancient times until the present day. There have always been people, who had the desire to go within, beyond the mind, and to discover who and what they are, and attain a higher spiritual consciousness.

During meditation the mind often wanders away, and the meditator has to be constantly vigilant and bring the attention back again and again. This of course involves some effort in the beginning, but as one gains proficiency, less effort will be necessary. When one is advanced on the path, keeping the mind calm and free from distracting thoughts can become a habit.

In it higher forms, meditation aims to free the mind from the subconscious compulsive habit to think incessantly. This leads to inner peace, inner freedom, and to awareness of one's real essence—The Inner I—The Spirit, which is above and beyond the mind. It also leads to serenity, clarity and bliss. In this sense, meditation means 'a cessation of the thought process'. It leads to quietening of the endless chatter of the mind.

Meditation is practiced in both the East and the West in its various forms. You don't need to be a monk or a hermit or live in seclusion or in an ashram in order to practice it. In fact, you can continue living your day-to-day life, have a job, a husband or a wife and kids, and still practice it. You don't need to follow any particular religion, wear special clothes or lead a certain lifestyle. Meditation is an inner activity, which can be practiced anywhere, and has nothing to do with any external way of life.

There are many techniques and traditions, some involve visualization and others the repetition of a mantra. Some techniques require contemplating on the meaning of selected verses from the scriptures, and others require focusing the attention on the breath, a candle or a certain shape. There are also techniques that require silencing the mind and becoming aware of the inner Self-within.

Though there are many techniques, meditation may be divided into two main forms. One involves thinking and focusing on a certain thought, idea or ideal, and the other, which is a more advanced form, requires the emptying of the mind of all thoughts and entering into a state of inner silence. It is not a state of dullness or unconsciousness, but a state of deep inner peace and awareness of one's real being.

Meditation has nothing to do with being lazy, impractical or dreamy. In order to practice it successfully, at least some degree of concentration ability is required, as well as self-discipline, willpower and perseverance, and the willingess to devote time, effort and energy to master it.

Regular practice of meditation affects in a positive way one's behaviour, thinking, state of mind and attitude, as well as one's health. It also develops patience, tolerance and tranquility, as well as self-mastery, discipline and inner strength, but in order to reap the rewards, it needs to be practiced regularly.

Tips for Meditation

Below you will find several things you can do to improve your ability to meditate, mitigate the inner resistance of the mind, and improve your chances of success. Read them attentively, and apply them to any technique that you practice.

1. It is important to meditate every day.
2. Keep up a positive attitude.
3. Do not meditate when you are tired.
4. Meditate in a place where you can be alone and undisturbed.

5. Sit in a comfortable position with your spine erect. You can sit on the floor, on a cushion or on a chair.
6. Relax your body.
7. Take a few slow deep breaths.
8. To relax even more, for a few moments focus on a pleasant memory, or a mental image of a place that makes you feel calm.
9. Think for a few moments about the benefits of meditation, how it will strengthen your focus, calm down your mind, ease stress and tension, etc.
10. Before you start to meditate, tell yourself that all thoughts, ideas and plans will have now to wait until you finish, and that nothing is going to distract your mind.
11. Start meditating calmly, yet with focused attention. The more focused the attention is, the easier it is to ignore thoughts and other distractions.
12. Strive to stay calm, both mentally and physically, and do not tense your body.
13. Patience, perseverance and self discipline should be always cultivated.
14. 10 minutes of practice are quite enough for a beginner.
15. Start with a simple technique. Here are two examples:
    (a) *Focus your attention on your incoming and outgoing breath.* For a few minutes, focus your attention on your breath. Breathe normally, while focusing on the act of breathing in and breathing out. Be careful not to strain your breath and your body.
    (b) *Focusing on an inspiring quote.* Choose an inspiring quote from any spiritual teacher, and

repeat it in your mind, trying to find its deep meaning, beyond the written words.

Meditation: Benefits and Goals

Regular meditation calms down the restlessness of the mind, and decreases the number of distracting thoughts, bringing a sense of inner peace and relaxation. As the sense of inner peace increases, the ability to concentrate and focus the mind improves.

With a peaceful mind one makes less mistakes, makes better judgments and decisions and becomes more patient and tolerant. This of course improves one's relationships with family, friends, neighbors and colleagues.

The benefits of meditation do not end here. Regular practice enhances the sense of happiness and contentment. As the mind becomes more and more peaceful, the number of worries, anxieties, fears and negative thoughts decreases, and in their absence, happiness rises unobstructed from within.

Much of the stress and tension we normally experience comes from our mind, and many problems, including ill health, are brought about or aggravated by stress and tension. This stress and tension can be reduced by regular meditation. When the mind is at peace, many problems just disappear, and others are more easily dealt with.

An undisciplined mind accepts every passing thought, and wastes one's time and energy on futile, useless or negative thoughts. It also often aggravates every problem and takes it out of proportion. With a disciplined and trained mind, this tendency gradually gets weaker, and may even disappear.

In time, one can see changes in the behavior and attitude and manner of thinking. The mind becomes more positive and one learns to react more constructively, patiently and calmly to the various situations of daily life, from dealing with people to dealing with problems, tasks or goals. One's actions become positive and efficient, focused and more satisfactory.

The benefits of meditation manifest on the physical, emotional, mental and spiritual levels. Some of them appear quite fast, and others take some more time. This depends on the amount of time devoted to practising it, the levels of earnestness and concentration, and on the inner ripeness of the meditating person. It is not enough to meditate once a week or once in a few days. Regular daily practice is required for attaining results.

There is evidence of the many rewards of regular meditation from people who meditate, and also from researches of scientists. Here are some of them:

Physical Benefits

- A deeper level of relaxation.
- Deep rest accompanied by decreased metabolic rate and lower heart rate.
- Decreased high blood pressure.
- Improved flow of air to the lungs.
- Increased levels of energy.
- Decreased muscle tension.
- More easily falling asleep and sleeping soundly.
- Improved state of the immune system.

Mental and Emotional Benefits

- Decrease in restless thinking.
- Increased ability to stay calm in every situation.
- Greater creativity.

- Decreased anxiety.
- Decreased depression.
- Decreased nervousness, irritability and moodiness.
- Enhancement of self-confidence.
- Improved concentration.
- Increased self-discipline.
- Improved learning ability and memory.
- Increased feelings of vitality.
- Enhanced feelings of happiness.
- More emotional stability.
- Developed intuition.

Spiritual Benefits

- Peace of mind.
- Emotional and mental detachment.
- Heightened awareness of the inner self.
- The ability to look within, beyond the body, mind and personality.
- Discovery of the power and consciousness beyond the ego.
- Discovery of one's true being.
- Attaining self-realization and spiritual awakening.

Meditation—The Antidote for Worries

Meditation has always been recognized as the antidote and remedy for tension, worry and fear. It is not a magical medicine, and results do not show overnight, but they are assured if you commit yourself to meditate each day.

We are living in a world full of tensions and worries. Work, relationships, financial conditions, health, dangers and fears provide enough fuel for tension and worries. They prevent inner peace, produce toxics in the body, injure the health and disturb life. They weaken both mind and body, and bring all kinds of problems.

The mind and the body need something to relax and calm them down, and this is one of the roles of meditation. Its effects last not only during the actual period devoted to it, but throughout the whole day, but for that to happen it has to be practiced earnestly and correctly for some time.

You might find it is difficult to start to meditate, because you do not have the motivation to do so, and you feel the need for proof of the benefits of meditation before you begin. The best proof you can gather is through your personal, direct experience. It is good to read about other people's experiences, but it is much better to gain first hand experience.

If you approach meditation with interest and love you will develop the patience and persistence necessary for success. Soon the twenty minutes will extend to thirty minutes and even longer. As in every other area, here too, when you start to see results your ambition and desire to succeed would grow.

There are many meditation techniques, and you may follow any one that attracts you, and with which you feel comfortable. Do not force yourself to do something that you do not like to do. This produces tension, which you are trying to avoid.

After practising for some time you will see how your inner peace level grows, and situations that previously caused you worry and tension lose their power to affect you. You will find that physical, emotional and mental tensions gradually start to diminish, and the door to peace of mind opens for you.

The process of meditating gradually takes your mind, thoughts and senses away from your immediate environment. The flow of stimulus from the environment and mind diminishes gradually, and both mind and body relax. This affects the metabolism of the body, cleanses it from toxics, and provides renewed energy and peace of mind.

Meditation is the antidote for tensions, fears and worries that most people go through. Its accumulated effects make it easier to stay calm under difficult situations, and thus get over them or steer away from them. It gives you not only peace of mind, but it also increases your inner strength, willpower and self discipline. It is an important tool for a happier and more relaxed life for everyone, no matter where he lives and what he does.

6

HOW TO DEVELOP WILLPOWER AND SELF-DISCIPLINE?

The possession of willpower and self-discipline or their lack, plays an important role in everyone's life. For example, you wish to go for a walk, knowing how good it is for your health and how wonderful you feel afterwards, but you feel too lazy, and prefer to watch TV instead. You might be aware of the fact that you need to change your eating habits or stop smoking, but you don't have the inner power and persistence to change these habits. Does this sound familiar? How many times have you said, "I wish I had willpower and self-discipline"? How many times have you started to do something, only to quit after a short while? We all have had experiences like these.

Everyone possesses some addictions or habits they wish they could overcome, such as smoking, excessive eating, laziness, procrastination or lack of assertiveness. To overcome these habits or addictions, one needs some degree of *willpower and self-discipline*. They make a great difference in everyone's life, and bring inner strength, self-mastery and decisiveness.

DEFINITIONS OF WILLPOWER AND SELF-DISCIPLINE

Willpower is the ability to overcome laziness and procrastination. It is the ability to control or reject unnecessary or harmful impulses. It is the ability to arrive at a decision and follow it with perseverance until its successful accomplishment. It is the inner power that overcomes the desire to indulge in unnecessary and useless habits, and the inner strength that overcomes inner emotional and mental resistance for taking action. It is one of the corner stones of success, both spiritual and material.

Self-discipline is the companion of willpower. It endows with the stamina to persevere in whatever one does. It bestows the ability to withstand hardships and difficulties, whether physical, emotional or mental. It grants the ability to reject immediate satisfaction, in order to gain something better, but, which requires effort and time.

Everyone has inner, unconscious, or partly conscious impulses, making them say or do things they later regret saying or doing. On many occasions people do not think before they talk or act. By developing these two powers, one becomes conscious of the inner, subconscious impulses, and gains the ability to reject them when they are not for his/her own good.

Willpower and self-discipline—these two powers help us to choose our behaviour and reactions, instead of being ruled by them. Their possession won't make life dull or boring. On the contrary, you will feel more powerful, in charge of yourself and your surroundings, happy and satisfied.

How many times have you felt too weak, lazy or shy to do something you wanted to do? You can gain inner strength, initiative and the ability to make decisions and follow them. Believe me, it is not difficult to develop these two powers. If you are earnest and are willing to become stronger, you will certainly succeed.

There is a misconception in the public mind regarding willpower. It is erroneously thought to be something strenuous and difficult, and that one has to exert and tense the body and mind when expressing it. It is a completely wrong concept. This is one of the reasons why people avoid using it, though they are conscious of its benefits. They acknowledge the fact that the employment of willpower in their life and affairs will greatly help them, and that they need to strengthen it, yet they do nothing about it.

Willpower gets stronger by holding back and not allowing the expression of unimportant, unnecessary and unhealthy thoughts, feelings, actions and reactions. If this saved energy is not allowed expression, it is stored inside you like a battery, and it becomes available at the time of need. By practising appropriate exercises, you develop your powers the same way, as a person who trains his/her muscles in order to strengthen them.

DEVELOPING WILLPOWER AND SELF-DISCIPLINE

An effective method for developing and improving these abilities is to perform certain actions or activities, which you would rather avoid doing due to laziness, procrastination, weakness, shyness, etc. Doing things that you usually do not like to do or feel too lazy to do, you overcome your subconscious resistance, train your mind to obey you, strengthen your inner powers and gain inner strength. Muscles get stronger by resisting the power of the barbells. Inner strength is attained by overcoming inner resistance. Remember, strengthening one of these abilities, automatically strengthens the other one.

Here are some exercises:

1. You are sitting in a bus or train and an old man or woman, or a pregnant lady walks in. Stand up and give up your seat, even if you prefer to stay seated. Act so, not just because it is polite, but because you are doing something that you are reluctant to do. This is an exercise in overcoming the resistance of your body, mind and feelings.
2. There are dishes in the sink that need washing, and you postpone washing them for later. Get up and wash them now. Do not let your laziness overcome you. When you know that in this way you are developing your willpower, and if you are convinced of the importance of willpower in your life, it will be easier for you to do whatever you have to do.
3. You come home tired from work and sit in front of the T.V., because you feel too lazy and too tired to take a shower first. Do not succumb to the desire to sit in front of the T.V, and go and take a shower.
4. You may know your body needs some physical exercise, but instead you keep on sitting doing nothing or watching a movie. Get up and walk, run or do some other physical exercise.
5. Do you like your coffee with sugar? If you do, then for one whole week drink it without sugar. Do you drink three cups of coffee each day? If you do, then drink only two cups a day for one whole week.
6. Sometimes, when you want to say something that is not important, decide not to say it.
7. Don't read some unimportant gossip in the newspaper, even if you want to.
8. You have a desire to eat something not too healthy. For the sake of the exercise refuse the desire.

9. If you find yourself-thinking unimportant, unnecessary, negative thoughts, try to develop a lack of interest in them, by thinking about their futility and uselessness.
10. Overcome your laziness. Convince yourself of the importance of what is to be done. Convince your mind that you gain inner strength when you act and do things, in spite of laziness, reluctance or senseless inner resistance.

Never say that you cannot follow the above exercises, because you certainly can. Be persistent no matter what. Motivate yourself by thinking about of the importance of performing the exercises, and the inner power and strength you will gain.

Trying to attempt too many exercises when you are still a beginner, might end in disappointment. It is better to start with a few easy exercises at first, and then gradually increase their number and move to the more difficult exercises.

Most of these exercises can be practiced anywhere and at anytime, which means that you don't have to devote special times for them. They will help you develop your willpower and self-discipline, enabling you to use them whenever you need them.

If you practice weight lifting, running or aerobics, you strengthen your muscles, so that when you need to move or carry something heavy, for example, you have the strength for it. By studying Spanish each day, you will be able to speak Spanish when you travel to Spain. It is the same with willpower and self-discipline; by strengthening them, they become available for your use whenever you need them.

If for the sake of an exercise, you stop doing something that you usually do, and overcome the inner resistance concerning it, you may resume doing it, if it is not harmful. For example, if you love drinking orange juice, and for the sake of an exercise you switch to drinking apple juice, after doing so for some time, and after it makes no great difference to you, you may go back to drinking orange juice, if you still like it. The point here is to develop inner strength, not making life difficult for you or continue doing things you don't like to do.

You need willpower and self-discipline to control your thoughts, improve your concentration, and to become the boss of your mind. The stronger these skills are, the more inner strength you possess.

Being the master of your mind you enjoy inner peace and happiness. External events do not sway you, and circumstances have no power over your peace of mind. This might sound too unreal for you, but experience will prove to you that all the above is true.

These skills are vital for achieving success. They give you more control over your life, help you change and improve habits, and are essential for self-improvement, spiritual growth and meditation.

THE FIVE PILLARS OF SELF-DISCIPLINE

The five pillars of self-discipline are: Acceptance, Willpower, Hard Work, Industry, and Persistence. If you take the first letter of each word, you get the acronym "A WHIP"—a convenient way to remember them, since many people associate self-discipline with whipping themselves into shape.

Self-discipline is the ability to get yourself to take action regardless of your emotional state.

Imagine what you could accomplish if you could simply get yourself to follow through on your best intentions no matter what. Picture yourself saying to your body, "You're overweight. Lose 10kg." Without self-discipline that intention won't become manifest. But with sufficient self-discipline, it's a done deal. The pinnacle of self-discipline is when you reach the point that when you make a conscious decision, it's virtually guaranteed you'll follow through on it.

Self-discipline is one of many personal development tools available to you. Of course it is not a panacea. Nevertheless, the problems which self-discipline can solve are important, and while there are other ways to solve these problems, self-discipline absolutely shreds them. Self-discipline can empower you to overcome any addiction or lose any amount of weight. It can wipe out procrastination, disorder, and ignorance. Within the domain of problems it can solve, self-discipline is simply unmatched. Moreover, it becomes a powerful team-mate when combined with other tools like passion, goal-setting, and planning.

Building Self-Discipline

Self-discipline is like a muscle. The more you train it, the stronger you become. The less you train it, the weaker you become. Just as everyone has different muscular strength, we all possess different levels of self-discipline. Everyone has some—if you can hold your breath a few seconds, you have some self-discipline. But not everyone has developed their discipline to the same degree.

Just as it takes muscle to build muscle, it takes self-discipline to build self-discipline.

The way to build self-discipline is analogous to using progressive weight training to build muscle. This means lifting weights that are close to your limit. Note that when you weight train, you lift weights that are within your ability to lift. You push your muscles until they fail, and then you rest.

Similarly, the basic method to build self-discipline is to tackle challenges that you can successfully accomplish but which are near your limit. This doesn't mean trying something and failing at it every day, nor does it mean staying within your comfort zone. You will gain no strength trying to lift a weight that you cannot budge, nor will you gain strength lifting weights that are too light for you. You must start with weights/challenges that are within your current ability to lift but which are near your limit.

Progressive training means that once you succeed, you increase the challenge. If you keep working out with the same weights, you won't get any stronger. Similarly, if you fail to challenge yourself in life, you won't gain any more self-discipline.

Just as most people have very weak muscles compared to how strong they could become with training, most people are very weak in their level of self-discipline.

It's a mistake to try to push yourself too hard when trying to build self-discipline. If you try to transform your entire life overnight by setting dozens of new goals for yourself and expecting yourself to follow through consistently starting the very next day, you're almost certain to fail. This is like a person going to the gym for the first time ever and packing 140 kg on the bench press. You will only look silly.

If you can only lift 10 lbs, you can only lift 10 lbs. There's no shame in starting where you are.

Similarly, if you're very undisciplined right now, you can still use what little discipline you have to build more. The more disciplined you become, the easier life gets. Challenges that were once impossible for you will eventually seem like child's play. As you get stronger, the same weights will seem lighter and lighter.

Don't compare yourself to other people. It won't help. You'll only find what you expect to find. If you think you're weak, everyone else will seem stronger. If you think you're strong, everyone else will seem weaker. There's no point in doing this. Simply look at where you are now, and aim to get better as you go forward.

Acceptance

The first of the five pillars of self-discipline is acceptance. Acceptance means that you perceive reality accurately and consciously acknowledge what you perceive.This may sound simple and obvious, but in practice it's extremely difficult. If you experience chronic difficulties in a particular area of your life, there's a strong chance that the root of the problem is a failure to accept reality as it is.

Why is acceptance a pillar of self-discipline? The most basic mistake people make with respect to self-discipline is a failure to accurately perceive and accept their present situation. Remember the analogy between self-discipline and weight training from yesterday's post? If you're going to succeed at weight training, the first step is to figure out what weights you can already lift. How strong are you right now? Until you figure out where you stand right now, you cannot adopt a sensible training programme.

If you haven't consciously acknowledged where you stand right now in terms of your level of self-discipline, it's highly unlikely that you're going to improve at all in this area. Imagine a would-be bodybuilder who has no idea how much weight she/he can lift and arbitrarily adopts a training routine. It's virtually certain that the chosen weights will be either too heavy or too light. If the weights are too heavy, the trainee won't be able to lift them at all and thus will experience no muscle growth.

And if the weights are too light, the trainee will lift them easily but won't build any muscle in doing so.

Similarly, if you want to increase your self-discipline, you must know where you stand right now. How strong is your discipline at this moment? Which challenges are easy for you, and which are virtually impossible for you?

Here's a list of challenges to get you thinking about where you stand right now (in no particular order):

- Do you shower/bathe every day?
- Do you get up at the same time every morning? Including weekends?
- Are you overweight?
- Do you have any addictions (caffeine, nicotine, sugar, etc.) you'd like to break but haven't?
- Is your email inbox empty right now?
- Is your office neat and well organized?
- Is your home neat and well organized?
- How much time do you waste in a typical day? On a weekend?
- If you make a promise to someone, what's the percentage chance you'll keep it?
- If you make a promise to yourself, what's the percentage chance you'll keep it?
- Could you fast for one day?
- How well organized is your computer's hard drive?
- How often do you exercise?
- What's the greatest physical challenge you've ever faced, and how long ago was it?
- How many hours of focused work do you complete in a typical workday?

— How many items on your to do list are older than 90 days?

— Do you have clear, written goals? Do you have written plans to achieve them?

— If you lost your job, how much time would you spend each day looking for a new one, and how long would you maintain that level of effort?

— How much TV do you currently watch? Could you give up TV for 30 days?

— How do you look right now? What does your appearance say about your level of discipline (clothes, grooming, etc)?

— Do you primarily select foods to eat based on health considerations or on taste/satiety?

— When was the last time you consciously adopted a positive new habit? Discontinued a bad habit?

— Are you in debt? Do you consider this debt an investment or a mistake?

— Did you decide in advance to be reading this blog right now, or did it just happen?

— Can you tell me what you'll be doing tomorrow? Next weekend?

— On a scale of 1-10, how would you rate your overall level of self-discipline?

— What more could you accomplish if you could answer that last question with a 9 or 10?

Just as there are different muscle groups which you train with different exercises, there are different areas of self-discipline: disciplined sleep, disciplined diet, disciplined work habits, disciplined communication, etc. It takes different exercises to build discipline in each area.

Progressive training works with self-discipline just as it does with building muscle. For example, if you can barely get out of bed at 10 am, are you likely to succeed at waking up at 5 am every morning? Probably not. But could you master getting up at 9:45 am? Very likely. And once you've done that, could you progress to 9:30 or 9:15? Sure. When I started getting up at 5am consistently, I had already done it several times for a few days in a row, and my normal wake-up time was 6-6:30 am, so that next step was challenging but achievable for me partly because I was already within range of it.

Without acceptance you get either ignorance or denial. With ignorance you simply don't know how disciplined you are—you've probably never even thought about it. You don't know that you don't know. You'll only have a fuzzy notion of what you can and can't do. You'll experience some easy successes and some dismal failures, but you're more likely to blame the task or blame yourself instead of simply acknowledging that the "weight" was too heavy for you and that you need to become stronger.

When you're in a state of denial about your level of discipline, you're locked into a false view of reality. You're either overly pessimistic or optimistic about your capabilities. And like the trainee who doesn't know his/her own strength, you won't get much better because it's unlikely you'll be able to hit the proper training zone by accident. On the pessimistic side, you'll only pick up easy weights and avoid the heavy ones which you could actually lift and which would make you stronger. And on the optimistic side, you'll keep trying to lift weights that are too heavy for you and failing, and afterwards you may either beat yourself up or resolve to try harder, neither of which will make you stronger.

Willpower

Willpower provides an intensely powerful yet temporary boost. Think of it as a one-shot thruster. It burns out quickly, but if directed intelligently, it can provide the burst you need to overcome inertia and create momentum.

Willpower is a concentration of force. You gather up all your energy and make a massive thrust forward. You attack your problems strategically at their weakest points until they crack, allowing you enough room to maneuver deeper into their territory and finish them off.

The application of willpower includes the following steps:

1. Choose your objective
2. Create a plan of attack
3. Execute the plan

With willpower you may take your time implementing steps 1 and 2, but when you get to step 3, you've got to hit it hard and fast.

Don't try to tackle your problems and challenges in such a way that a high level of willpower is required every day. Willpower is unsustainable. If you attempt to use it for too long, you'll burn out. It requires a level of energy that you can maintain only for a short period of time.

Hard Work

Most people will do what's easiest and avoid hard work—and that's precisely why you should do the opposite. The superficial opportunities of life will be attacked by hordes of people seeking what's easy. The much tougher challenges will usually see a lot less competition and a lot more opportunity. When you discipline yourself to do what is hard, you gain access to a realm of results that are denied everyone else. The willingness to do what is difficult is like having a key to a special private treasure room.

The nice thing about hard work is that it's universal. It doesn't matter what industry you're in—hard work can be used to achieve positive long-term results regardless of the specifics.

Hard work pays off. When someone tells you otherwise, beware the sales pitch for something "fast and easy" that's about to come next. The greater your capacity for hard work, the more rewards fall within your grasp. The deeper you can dig, the more treasure you can potentially find.

Being healthy is hard work. Finding and maintaining a successful relationship is hard work. Raising kids is hard work. Getting organized is hard work. Setting goals, making plans to achieve them, and staying on track is hard work. Even being happy is hard work (true happiness that comes from high self-esteem, not the fake kind that comes from denial and escapism).

Hard work goes hand-in-hand with acceptance. One of the things you must accept are those areas of your life that won't succumb to anything less than hard work. Perhaps you've had no luck finding a fulfilling relationship. Maybe the only way it's going to happen is if you accept you're going to have to do what you've been avoiding. Perhaps you want to lose weight. Maybe it's time to accept that the path to your goal requires disciplined diet and exercise. Perhaps you want to increase your income. Maybe you should accept that the only way it will happen is with a lot of hard work.

Your life will reach a whole new level when you stop avoiding and fearing hard work and simply surrender to it. Make it your ally instead of your enemy. It's a potent tool to have on your side.

Industry

Industry is working hard. In contrast to hard work, being

industrious doesn't necessarily mean doing work that's challenging or difficult. It simply means putting in the time. You can be industrious doing easy work or hard work. Imagine you have a baby. You'll spend a lot of time changing diapers. But that isn't really hard work—it's just a matter of doing it over and over many times each day.

In life there are many tasks that aren't necessarily difficult, but they collectively require a significant time investment. If you don't discipline yourself to stay on top of them, they can make a big mess of your life. Just think of all the little things you need to do: shopping, cooking, cleaning, laundry, taxes, paying bills, home maintenance, childcare, etc. And this is just for home—if you include work the list grows even longer. These things may not reach your A-list for importance, but they still need to be done.

Self-discipline requires that you develop the capacity to put in the time where it's needed. A lot of messes are created when we refuse to put in the time to do what needs to be done—and to do it correctly. Such messes range from a messy desk or cluttered email inbox all the way down to an Enron or Worldcom. Big mess or small mess—take your pick. Either way a significant contributing factor is the refusal to do what needs to be done.

Sometimes it's clear what needs to be done. Sometimes it isn't clear at all. But ignoring the mess won't help no matter what. If you don't know what needs to be done, the first step is to figure it out. This may require you to seek out information and educate yourself.

Disciplining yourself to be industrious allows you to squeeze more value out of your time. Time is a constant, but your personal productivity is not. Some people will use the hours of their day far more efficiently than others. It's amazing that people will spend extra money to buy a faster computer or a fuel efficient car, but they'll barely pay any attention to their personal capacity. Your personal productivity will do a lot more for you than a computer or a car in the long run. Give an industrious programmer a 10-year old computer, and she/he'll get much more done with it over the course of a year than a lazy programmer with state of the art technology.

Despite all the technology and gadgets we have available that can potentially make us more efficient, your personal productivity is still your greatest bottleneck. Don't look to technology to make you more productive. If you don't consider yourself productive without technology, you won't be productive with it—it will only serve to mask your bad habits. But if you're already industrious without technology, it can help you become even more so. Think of technology as a force multiplier—it multiplies what you already are.

When you pursue the path of developing your personal productivity, it may cause you some days of hair-pulling and teeth-gnashing, but it does eventually pay off. Many people are attracted to the idea of becoming more productive out of basic common sense. It doesn't take much brainpower to figure out that if you use your time more efficiently, you'll complete more tasks, and therefore you'll accumulate results faster. Personal productivity allows you to create enough space in your life to do all the things you feel you should be doing: eat healthy, exercise, work hard, deepen relationships, have a wonderful social life, and make a difference. Otherwise, something has to give. Without a high level of personal productivity, you'll likely have to give up something that's important to you. You have conflicts between health and work, work and family, family and friends. Industry can give you the ability to enjoy all of these things, so you don't have to choose work over family or vice versa. You can have both.

Of course industry is only one tool among many. It will allow you to complete your work efficiently, but it won't tell you what work to do in the first place. Industry is a low level tool. Working hard doesn't necessarily mean working smart. But this weakness of industry doesn't remove its powerful place in your personal development toolbox. Once you've decided on a course of action and see your plans laid out in front of you, nothing can do the job as well as industry. In the long run your results will come from your actions, and industry is all about action.

Persistence

Persistence is the ability to maintain action regardless of your feelings. You press on even when you feel like quitting.When you work on any big goal, your motivation will wax and wane like waves hitting the shore. Sometimes you'll feel motivated; sometimes you won't. But it's not your motivation that will produce results—it's your action. Persistence allows you to keep taking action even when you don't feel motivated to do so, and therefore you keep accumulating results.

Persistence will ultimately provide its own motivation. If you simply keep taking action, you'll eventually get results, and results can be very motivating. For example, you may become a lot more enthusiastic about dieting and exercising once you've lost those first 10 pounds and feel your clothes fitting more loosely.

Self-Discipline: Its Benefits and Importance

One of the main characteristics of self-discipline is the ability to forgo instant and immediate gratification and pleasure, in favour of some greater gain or more satisfying results, even if this requires effort and time. Self-discipline gives you the power to stick to your decisions and follow them through, without changing your mind, and is therefore one of the important requirements for achieving goals.

The possession of self-discipline enables you to choose, and then persevere with actions, thoughts and behaviour, which lead to improvement and success. It also gives you the power and inner strength to overcome addictions, procrastination and laziness and to follow through whatever you do.

This is a very useful and needed skill in everyone's life, and though most people acknowledge its importance, yet very few do anything to develop and strengthen it.

Contrary to common belief, self-discipline is not a severe and limited behavior or a restrictive lifestyle. It is a very important igredient for success, any form of success. It expresses itself as perseverance, the ability not to give up despite failure and setbacks, as self-control, and as the ability to resist temptations and distractions that tend to stand in the way of attaining aims and goals. In fact, it is one of the most important pillars of real and stable success.

This ability leads to self-confidence, self-esteem and inner strength, and consequently to happiness and satisfaction. On the other hand, lack of self-discipline may lead to failure, loss, health and relationships problems, obesity and to other troubles.

Life often presents challenges and problems on the path to success and achievement, and in order to rise above them you have to act with perseverance and persistence, and this requires self-discipline. You also this skill to cure and overcome eating disorders, addictions, smoking, drinking and other negative habits.

Self-discipline is vital for overcoming eating disorders, addictions, smoking, drinking and other negative habits. It is also an important requirement for studying and learning, for developing any skill, and for success in self-improvement, spiritual growth and meditation.

Most people acknowledge the importance and benefits of self-discipline, but very few take real steps to develop and strengthen it. This ability can be strengthened and developed like any other skill, through training. Yes, you can develop self-discipline with special exercises, which you can practice at any time and place.

WILLPOWER—YOUR INNER STRENGTH

Willpower is the inner strength and the inner engine that propels towards success and achievement. It is the power that pushes into action in every area of life. Willpower is one of the most important and desirable inner powers, and its lack or presence determines whether you will fail or accomplish your desires and ambitions and attain success.

Willpower is erroneously considered as a quality belonging only to highly successful people, who depend on strength and force to achieve their goals. The truth is that it can be developed by everyone, and it is important, useful and desirable in the small affairs of life, as it is in the achievement of major goals.

If you usually feel too lazy, developing your inner strength will help you to overcome this laziness. If you usually procrastinate, possess low self-esteem, feel weak and vulnerable or lack self-control, strengthening this power will help you too.

Willpower, which is inner strength, manifests as the ability to control unnecessary and harmful impulses. It also manifests as the ability to decide, abide by this decision, and follow it with perseverance until its successful accomplishment. This ability gives you the courage and strength to endure and overcome inner and outer resistance and opposition, difficulties and hardships.

There are many who lack the inner strength to say "no". Others find it difficult to follow and assert their ideas and beliefs. Some are afraid to take action and make changes or they lack resolution and the persistence to go on with their plans to the end. A strong power of the will can change all this.

It is the right and privilege of everyone to develop this ability. Everyone can develop it to a greater or smaller extent, depending on the desire, earnestness, ambition and time devoted to developing and strengthening this inner power.

You do not require super ordinary powers to develop it. You do not need to sleep on a bed of nails, fast or stand on one foot for days, as Yogis do. The concept that the development of willpower requires you to undergo suffering and physical mutilation is not true.

Developing willpower and inner strength is a gradual process that everyone can undertake. Some will be able to reach higher levels of power, while others will reach different degrees of development, but the way is open to all.

You will have to give up some unnecessary and harmful pleasures and change some unhealthy habits, but this is for a higher good. You give up something harmful or useless, in order to gain strength and power that will help you in every area of your life. In fact, the whole process can be turned into an absorbing, enjoyable and interesting challenge.

Training and exercising your willpower will fill you with strength, courage, and assertiveness. As your power grows, it will be easier for you to get rid of habits and attitudes that stand in your way to a better life. You will gain inner strength that will help you at your job and at home, in your relationships, with carrying on your tasks and with accomplishing your ambitions.

How to Develop Your Inner Strength

Most people are not are not born with inner strength, but it can be developed like any other skill. Inner strength consists of willpower, self-discipline, self-control, persistence, detachment, the ability to concentrate and peace of mind. Let us focus on two of the ingredients, willpower and self-discipline. These skills are important and essential tools for success in all areas of life. They can be learned and developed like any other skill, yet, in spite of this, only few take any steps to develop and strengthen them in a systematic way.

Willpower is the inner strength to make decisions, take action, and handle and execute any aim or task, regardless of inner and outer resistance, discomfort or difficulties. It manifests as the ability to overcomes laziness, temptations and negative habits, and to carry out actions, even if they require effort, are unpleasant and tedious or are contrary to one's habits.

Self-discipline is the ability to reject instant gratification or pleasure in favor of something better or a higher goal. It manifests as the inner strength to stick to actions or plans in spite of obstacles, difficulties or unpleasantness. It is one of the pillars of success, and bestows the inner strength to direct your energy and attention to your goal, and persevere until it is accomplished.

Both of these skills are required for the efficient handling of all activities and decisions. They are required for doing a good job, for success in business, for studying, losing weight, exercising, maintaining good relationships, changing habits, self-improvement, meditation, spiritual growth, keeping promises and for almost everything else.

There are simple and effective methods for developing these powers and attaining inner strength:

1. Refusing to satisfy unimportant or unhealthy desires.
2. Doing things that are useful, but which you resist doing.

By overcoming inner resistance you develop inner power and strength.

By refusing and rejecting useless, harmful or unnecessary desires and actions, and sometimes intentionally acting contrary to your habits, you sharpen and strengthen your inner strength. You get stronger through constant practice, just like exercising your muscles at a gym makes your muscles stronger. In both cases, when you need inner power or physical strength, they are available and are at your disposal.

Here are a few exercises to strengthen your inner powers that use ordinary day-to-day activities:

- Don't read the newspaper for a few days.
- Now and then drink your coffee or tea without sugar.
- Climb up the stairs instead of taking the lift.
- Park you car a little farther away from you destination, so that you have to walk.
- Now and then choose not to watch one of your favourite TV programmes.
- Read a book that is useful and informative, but which you find boring.
- Curb your desire to criticize people.
- Delay your desire to retort angrily.
- Try to get out of bed quickly on a cold day.

These are only a few examples to show you how you can develop your inner strength. By practising these or similar exercises you gain inner power, which you can use when you are in need of it. By practising them you develop your inner muscles, just like lifting barbells develops your physical muscles.

Making Resolutions

Real willpower has nothing to do with making emotional resolutions. These are two completely different things. There is a common misunderstanding of what willpower means, and it is often confused with doings things emotionally.

Sometimes, in response to certain situations or events, we suddenly desire to follow a certain activity, goal or desire, and we enthusiastically and emotionally start doing something about it. The problem is that after a while the emotions calm down, and we quit what we have started, since we lack enough inner power and strength to proceed.

We often make resolutions and promises to do something, behave in a particular way, study, look for a job or a partner and so on, and we might even start acting according to our resolutions, but this goes on only for a short while. We start with much noise, but end in silence. We make resolutions enthusiastically and optimistically, but then we lose our enthusiasm and stop doing what we promised ourselves to do.This kind of behavior weakens the power of the will, and makes us lose faith in our ability to use our willpower. Then we might even start believing that willpower is just a myth, an unreal thing. This is an erroneous idea, because no real willpower was involved here.

As said earlier, most of the resolutions that people make are triggered by emotions. They make them in response to some strong emotion or thought, and rarely because of common sense and reasonable, balanced thinking. The driving powers behind these resolutions are feelings and emotions, but feelings and emotions are not stable and not constant. One moment you might feel you can conquer the world, and a moment later you may feel weak and incompetent, and everything seems so impossible to do.

A resolution made on the spur of the moment is usually useless. The emotion that triggered it might disappear a short while later, and there will be no desire left to carry on the resolution. Another important point to mention is that subconscious habits are stronger than any resolution, and they usually overcome any decision and desire for change.

All this leads people to believe that they lack willpower, and to regard it as unreal, as an illusion, but this is not so. No willpower has been involved in such resolutions, just temporary emotions and desires. Real willpower is something utterly different. It is not gained in a day, but requires training over a period of time. You cannot expect a physically weak person to lift heavy weight, but if he trains himself regularly, he will get stronger. It is the same with the strengthening of the power of the will.

Real willpower is not dependent on feelings, emotions, temporary enthusiasm or optimism. It is an ability that is developed over a period of time and can turn into a habit. After developing it, you will be able to use it whenever and wherever required.

Training of the will also develops self-discipline, as both abilities are interconnected. Such training also develops concentration, perseverance, assertiveness, self-confidence and the inner strength to make decisions with a balanced, calm mental attitude, and carry them out until their successful fulfilment. You become conscious of a wonderful inner power, which is an inseparable part of you.

Constant training of the power of the will results in a real power, which is always available. It is not the same as programming the mind to do one particular action, and then, when you need to do something else, you start again programming the mind for that other action. Real willpower is like a master key, once present, it can be applied to any sort of action or decision.

7

HOW TO GET MOTIVATED?

Motivation is a driving force. In order to accomplish anything, you need a driving force, otherwise nothing will happen. A wish is not strong enough to make you take action. A wish is a weak desire. Only a strong desire can drive forward, to act and accomplish aims and goals. In order to get motivated, you need to know exactly what it is that you want, to possess a strong desire, and to be willing to do whatever it takes to accomplish your goal.

More than often there is lack of motivation or only a short-lived one. How many times have you started enthusiastically a weight loss programme, began a body building or aerobics training programme or started to learn a foreign language, only to stop after a short while? Few people possess enough willpower and self-discipline to go through to the end with what they begin.

It easier to show motivation in connection with a subject that is dear to you. If you desire something, but you don't feel motivated enough to act, this means that the desire is not important enough. To be motivated to take action and do something in respect to your desire, you need to possess a really strong desire. Motivation has much to do with the emotions and the imagination, which means that if you want to increase it, you have to work on your feelings and imagination.

Often, a person has the desire and ambition to get something done or achieve a certain goal, but lacks the push, the initiative and the willingness to take action. This is due to lack of motivation and inner drive. Motivation strengthens the ambition, increases initiative and gives direction, courage, energy and the persistence to follow one's goals. A motivated person takes action and does whatever it needs to achieve his/her goals.

Motivation becomes strong when you have a vision, a clear mental image of what you want to achieve, and also a strong desire to materialize it. In this situation motivation awakens and pushes you forward, toward taking action and making the vision a reality.

Motivation can be applied to every action and goal. There could be motivation to study a foreign language, to get good grades at school, bake a cake, write a poem, take a walk every day, make more money, get a better job, buy a new house, own a business, or become a writer, a doctor or a lawyer. Motivation is present whenever there is a clear vision, precise knowledge of what one wants to do, a strong desire and faith in one's abilities.

Motivation is one of the most important keys to success. When there is lack of motivation you either get no results, or only mediocre results, whereas when there is motivation you attain greater and better results and achievements. Compare a student who lacks motivation and who hardly studies, to a student who is highly motivated, and who devotes many hours to his studies; they will get absolutely different grades.

Lack of motivation shows lack of enthusiasm, zest and ambition, whereas the possession of motivation is a sign of strong desire, energy and enthusiasm, and the willingness to do whatever it takes to achieve what one sets out to do. A motivated person is a happier person, more energetic, and sees the positive end result in his/her mind.

IMPACTS OF LACK OF MOTIVATION AND ENTHUSIASM

Motivation and enthusiasm manifest as desire and interest, and as a driving force that pushes to take action and pursue goals. Lack of motivation and enthusiasm denotes absence or deficiency in desire, interest and driving force.

Lack of motivation and lack of enthusiasm are two of the main reasons for failure and of living a mediocre life. People lacking in motivation and enthusiasm are usually passive, blame everything and everyone for their circumstances, and often come up with many excuses why they shouldn't or cannot do this or that. On the other hand, a motivated person is energetic and positive, takes action to improve his or her life, and does not give up when there are problems.

Lack of motivation and enthusiasm can show up everywhere, at home, at work, in relationships, in pursuing goals and in everything else. This often brings indifference, unhappiness and dissatisfaction.

What are the reasons for lack of motivation and enthusiasm?

- Lack of faith in one's abilities.
- Fear of failure, due to failure in the past.
- Low self-esteem.
- Lack of enough interest.
- Fear of what others might say.
- The habit of procrastination.
- Laziness.
- No awareness of the importance and usefulness of the subject or goal.
- The feeling or belief that there are other more important things to do.

— Not having the time to delve into the subject or goal.

— Being too stressed or nervous.

— Absence of enough stimuli or incentives.

The above mentioned reasons stifle motivation and enthusiasm, and are only excuses for not acting. However, you learn to overcome and disregard them, by becoming aware of them, acknowledging them, and understanding that you can change the programming of your mind.

Sometimes, people show short bursts of motivation or enthusiasm. They start doing something enthusiastically, but lose interest and motivation after a while, because they find it hard to sustain them.

If you wish to improve your life, you need to awaken motivation and enthusiasm. You need to realize how much you lose by their absence, and how much you gain by having them.

If you are overweight, and you don't have enough inner strength to exercise your body or follow a diet, you should consider strengthening your motivation to lose weight.

If you are a student, and are too lazy to study, you need to strengthen your desire to invest more attention, time and energy in your studies.

If you are lonely and gloomy, but wish to have love and happiness in your life, you need to kindle your desire and enthusiasm to find love. You need to awaken the desire and willingness to put time and effort into searching for someone to share your life with.

You need incentive and drive for following your big dreams, and also for the performance of minor daily tasks and chores, otherwise, laziness, absence of energy and procrastination will set in. Instead of suffering, feeling uncomfortable and passive, it would be much better to produce enough motivation to take action and do things. This will make you feel much better, happy and satisfied.

Procrastination, laziness, indifference and passivity cause unhappiness, weakness and lack of satisfaction, but being enthusiastic, motivated and active bring a sense of joy, strength and power. By getting motivated, you act, do things, take your mind off problems and difficulties and focus on finding solutions and achieving success.

HOW TO GET MOTIVATED AND MORE ENTHUSIASTIC?

Find out where you really need motivation. This means finding out what really matters to you, what actions will bring benefits and improvement into your life and the life of the people around you.

Find what are your real goals in life, but don't forget also to focus your attention on the little things of life, where a little motivation will help too. You will feel better and your life would improve, if you also overcome lack of motivation in small everyday life matters, such as washing the dishes, throwing the garbage, cooking, cleaning, working, reading, writing a letter or just being nice to your neighbors.

Often people start practising concentration exercises, meditation, self-discipline exercises or any other programme relating to self-improvement or spiritual growth, but not seeing immediate and spectacular results, stop and give up. Everything in life requires some work, effort and time, and self-improvement or spiritual growth methods are no different.

The question is what to do when interest and enthusiasm wanes? How to persevere when there isn't enough willpower and self-discipline? The programme or goal might seems worthwhile, but there isn't enough inner strength to pursue them. Self-defeating habits, negative programming, and lack of inner strength stand on one's way.This is why people buy and read books, attend classes, courses and workshop, and yet find they are not making enough progress. This is why enthusiasm and hopes are replaced by depression, self-pity and lack of self-esteem.

Often, after reading a book or an article, after listening to a lecture or watching a movie, there is a burst of enthusiasm and a high energy level, but this often does not last long.

So what can you do to keep enthusiastic and motivated? Short spurts of enthusiasm or motivation are not enough to accomplish anything of value. You need to keep your desire and inner flame alive and focused on your goal. So what can you do about it?

— Devote 10 minutes a day to reading and thinking about the benefits of what you want to do or accomplish.

— Read every day about people who achieved success by being tenacious and persistent.

— Every day, find a quiet place, and for several minutes visualize yourself acting with enthusiasm and motivation.

— Every success requires dedication, time, perseverance and tenacity. This means that you should not give up quickly. There is a well known story about a gold prospector, who, after digging to some depth did not find anything, gave up and went away. Then someone else came, and after digging just a few inches more, struck gold. You need to be patient and persistent, even if you see no progress, because success might be just a few inches away.

- Keep repeating affirmations that empower you and inflame your enthusiasm and motivation.
- Never consider what you are doing as drudgery. With some thinking and some changes you can turn it into a pleasurable activity.
- Once you decide about anything, go on with it, even after you lose enthusiasm and desire. Don't give up, even if what you are doing seems to be like a burden and drudgery. Don't give up, even if you feel bored. Just keep telling yourself about the benefits of what you are doing, and keep thinking and visualizing how it will be like after accomplishing what you have set to do.

Remember, this is your own life, and you are responsible for it. Why succumb to laziness and negative programming? This might not be easy, and there might be obstacles on the way. Yet, keep thinking about how happy you would be after achieving success, and how your life would change, if you disregard laziness, negative thoughts, negative programming and the fear of hard and sustained work. You need to keep your mind on the goal, no matter what.

Don't rely on spurts of enthusiasm to carry you to your destination. You need to stand up, not give up, and awaken the dormant powers that are within you. Never give up, but keep going on, even if the going is tough and you feel the desire to quit. If you keep going, and use affirmations and visualizations, soon your desire and enthusiasm will grow and the progress will become easier.

SELF-MOTIVATION

What is self-motivation? It is key to the enjoyment of life. We can either sit and do nothing or we can get involved in life.

Self-motivation is a crucial element in getting the most out of life. What gets us up and moving. Trying, striving, stumbling, getting up, driving forward, achieving? Our self-motivation. We see something we like, need or want and we go for it. What self motivates us? Partly that which we go for and partly ourselves. We provide the enthusiasm, the effort, the thought, the impetus that kicks us into action.

What does it take to self-motivate ourselves and utilize this energy, this force? What is self-motivation? A few simple changes can get us on the road to success:

- *Balance in life*—between work, home, rest and play. If you want something, sometimes you need to simplify other areas of your life.
- *Leave the unnecessary behind.* Our emotions affect our behaviour and affect our ability to succeed. Go for what you want and then make it happen.
- *Concentrate.* Look at what you are doing, need to do. List your decisions, tasks, *goals*. This brings them into view. Prioritize them. Make some decisions. Set your tasks and goals. Work your plan.
- *Do what you can.* Seek help or assistance if required. Don't believe you can do everything yourself.

Getting organised is run of the first rungs of the ladder of self-motivation to your success.

So, which is it? Inspiration or Perspiration? Self-empowerment and self-motivation? Remember all the brilliant examples of the successful and famous. Those people who went through the wringer of perspiration and effort, sparked by their inspiration, belief and vision. That one day their idea, invention, book, whatever—could become a reality. Their trials and tribulations. Their successes, setbacks, rejections and failures. Yet they kept faith with themselves. They maintained their self-confidence. They utilized their positive mental attitude. Their self-motivation a key. They kept on going, when most would have walked away, and made their 'little' bit of history.

Belief in yourself is so precious. Respect yourself also. Utilize your talents supported by your values. Believe in your sense of self-worth. Be disciplined. Set goals. Adopt the behaviour of the successful person you are.

Being Self-motivated means driven, focused, ready for objective discussion, also being sharp and smart enough not to be manipulated and be open to positive learning. Being in this state of mind always, is the challenge. To help be motivated, try taping your exercises on your wall, keeping your calories on paper is good. If you do this you will be motivated to lose weight, because you will have constant reminders.

Positive Self-motivation

Positive Self-motivation is that personal inner drive to achieve and succeed. Motivation is what builds winners in life. A self-motivated person will run circles around one that lacks any type of personal drive.

To increase your motivation we must first take a look at your attitude. There is one thing you can be sure of, if you have a poor or negative attitude your motivation or personal drive to accomplish any task will be lacking.

Attitude is the established way of responding to people and situations that we have learned, based on the beliefs, values and assumptions we hold, and it is shown in every action we take.

Most tend to believe that their attitude is a reflection of their surroundings but it's actually your surroundings that is a direct reflection of your attitude.

If you have a negative attitude you will only attract more negativity into your life. You have heard the old saying: "Misery Loves Company," well that is exactly how it works with your attitude. If you have a negative attitude the only type of people that will want to be around you will be those that are equally or even more negative then yourself.

You can choose to be motivated a little bit or a lot, it actually takes motivation to even make the choice. However there are two types of motivation, first you have positive self-motivation and you have negative motivation.

One who has positive self-motivation wakes up in the morning and looks at the day ahead optimistically. A self-motivated person thinks of every new day as a new opportunity, a day full of promising challenges and positive achievements.

Then you have the negative motivation and that is the person who wakes up in the morning and looks upon the day ahead as one filled with problems and not challenges, they can only think about getting through the day and they never focus on the positive achievements. This is the person that gripes and complains about everything and they think the world is conspiring against them and that is why they fail to live up to their true potential.

People tend to believe that they have no control over their attitude but nothing could be farther from the truth. You have to learn how to not allow your current situation to take hold of your attitude. Bad times will always pass but if you dwell upon them it will only extend the time it takes for them to pass.

Self-motivation is having the strength to keep pushing forward even when things are tough. If you really want to excel in life you need to be highly self-motivated and a positive attitude will give you the personal strength to keep pushing forward no matter how difficult their current circumstance may be.

You have to constantly ask yourself what are you presenting to the world right now and if you don't have a smile on your face and warm feelings in your heart then you pretty much have your answer.

This is where your personal self-motivation comes into play. Developing or displaying the strength of character to change a negative attitude you are presenting to those around you is a clear sign of positive self-motivation.

If you feel miserable inside it is going to show to all those around you. You must begin to focus on the good things in life and stop wasting your time with such self-destructive feelings.

You have the control to change how you feel and how you present yourself to the rest of the world. Wouldn't you rather put your energy into developing a positive attitude instead of digging a deeper hole of despair?

When you motivate yourself to take control of your feelings and you become determined to focus your mind on only positive events or situations you will improve every relationship you have in your life.

Living with a positive attitude and outlook toward life will draw more positive people and circumstances into your life. It really is an incredible power that we all possess, the power to control our inner being.

Always be aware that your inner world becomes a mirror of your outer world and the more pleasant you present yourself to others the more they will enjoy your company.

To draw upon your personal positive self-motivation to overcome negative thoughts and feelings is the characteristic of a real winner in life.

Empower yourself with positive thinking and turn negative motivation into positive and productive self-motivation. Maintaining a positive attitude will brighten everyday and you will no longer wake up in the morning with a feeling of dread, instead you will awake with a spirit of joy and you will look upon the day ahead with positive expectation. When you expect the best you are more likely to experience and achieve the best.

When you take these actions and you make real changes in your behaviour it becomes infectious to those around you. A happy, positive, outgoing person will just naturally draw happy, positive, outgoing people into their inner circle.

The best type of motivation is positive self-motivation, as that will always give you the personal drive to achieve and succeed whether your being encouraged or not.

There are some people that lack motivation all together and they have the real need for someone to get them moving almost on a daily basis.

Your attitude has everything to do with your self-motivation. Just try think of how you feel when your having a bad day and it just seems as though nothing is going your way.

You most likely are agitated and miserable, you cannot see the positive in anything so you lose the desire to do anything other than to mope around the house or lay on the couch and watch TV.

This is the perfect example of how your attitude affects your self-motivation, when your attitude is poor you lack the drive to do anything.

Now turn it around and visualize yourself as having a terrific day and a positive attitude about everything. When you do this can you see and feel how good you feel and how motivated you are to take on the challenges of the day ahead?

A lousy attitude and you lack self-motivation altogether but a strong, positive, joyful attitude brings along with it the personal drive to accomplish anything.

Tactics of Self-Motivation

The following motivation techniques and self-motivation techniques will help you to establish, maintain and strengthen motivation and incentive and help you to know how to motivate yourself in an effective way.

Motivational Power of Goals

Goals are a great source of motivation, as they help us to nurture our motivation and provide necessary focus and direction and should therefore be integrated into our "toolbox" of motivation techniques. Wise goals allow us to do "whatever necessary", which helps us to drastically increase our perseverance and our success-rate of accomplished goals. Perseverance is especially necessary once we set ourselves very ambitious goals. The utmost important aspect of an effective goal is that you have chosen it for yourself and that you really want to achieve it; so much that it will create a motivational desire within you and increase your incentive drastically.

Vision Board

Once you have set yourself some effective goals it is important to keep your goals in mind, as they will only motivate you as long as you don't forget these goals. In order to achieve this you should consider writing your goals down on a "goal list" that you read once or twice a day. The most effective solution to keep goals and aims in mind is to create a vision board that includes photos of all your goals you aspire to accomplish. A vision board strengthens motivation drastically, as it will be easier for you to associate more positive feelings with the goals in form of a picture than in form of a list of words. Make sure to place the vision board at some space where you will see it at least once or twice a day. Even better: place it in your home desk, office or to another place where you need to be motivated the most during a regular day.

Visualization

Motivational goals on will strengthen motivation, but in order to *peak motivation* you need to visualize your goals if you want to make sure to profit the most from motivational goals. Visualization is no rocket science as it only requires you to imagine a picture or "scene" of a desired outcome, e.g. the accomplishment of a goal. This helps you to strengthen your self-believe and furthermore prepares the mind to achieve your goals. Visualization techniques are so effective because our mind cannot differentiate between a real situation and a very intensive imagined experience.

Music

Music can be a fantastic motivator as it is able to elicit positive emotions within us, when chosen right it can even motivate us. Music could definitely be considered as the easiest motivation method when compared with the other motivation techniques. Lounge music, ballads or songs with a sad song text have no positive effect on our motivation, as they either create comfort, sadness, tiredness or even negative emotions within us. Music is the easiest, yet very effective, motivation techniques a person can integrate into his live. Once you have found some motivational songs you can listen to them during your ride to work to energize yourself for the upcoming day. In the following you will find some of the most motivational songs.

Visual Motivation

"A picture is worth a thousand words." This is a Chinese Proverb. It was already mentioned that pictures can strengthen motivation. Besides this you can also profit of motivational pictures, as they elicit within a view seconds very positive emotions when viewing them. You can either create a motivational picture for yourself that you associate motivational feelings with, or you can have a quick search on the internet for motivational posters.

Rewards

The process of linking a reward with a requirement is the most effective motivation method, above all other motivation techniques, as a reward allows you to associate positive feelings with the efforts you make to achieve a goal. Rewards sharpen your desire to achieve an objective, as you will only be presented with the reward when you accomplish the aim. A reward can be tremendously effective when we want to pursue very ambitious goals, as it helps us to develop perseverance and the attitude to do "whatever it takes" until the aim is accomplished.

Interest and Commitment

If you ever performed a task that you were highly interested in you will know of the benefits of true interest as a motivational factor. You might have felt committed to the task and have been driven by the desire to complete the task. If you are able to link commitment and interest to your tasks you will advance your motivation and strengthen your incentive. If you are facing a task that you really dislike and are not interested in you should try to identify what benefits you might be presented once you accomplish the task. Get an extra portion of motivation by visualizing the positive outcome once a task is finished! By doing so you can direct your focus on the positive aspects of a task, rather than thinking about the negative sides of it.

Integrate Motivation into Your Life

The previously mentioned motivation techniques allow you to either increase or strengthen motivation, but to keep your motivation on a constant and very high level we need to integrate motivation into our daily life. This can be achieved by identifying motivational aspects of your life and then to integrate these into your daily routine. Some people can motivate themselves by reading some motivational quotes, while others prefer to get motivated by exercising regularly. Whatever it is that motivates you: integrate it into your daily routine. Make a habit out of it! This could be for example to visualize your goals both in the morning and the evening, or to imagine all the beautiful aspects of your life while you are taking a shower.

Just Do It

One of the biggest obstacles to become motivated to perform a task is procrastination, the habit of postponement. Besides its negative influences on our motivation it can also cause regret and discouragement, which is not worthwhile. The next time you are confronted with a task that you do not really want to perform you should immediately take action and just do what needs to be done. This helps you to avoid procrastination and eliminates false hopes such as "waiting until motivation arises". You will see that the most difficult thing is to take action, but once you decided to execute a task you will find further motivation that keeps you going. If you noticed that you try to postpone especially tasks that seem to be very demanding or difficult it can be helpful to split this task into sub-tasks that you approach step by step. By accomplishing one sub-task after the other you will build momentum and advance your motivation.

A Motivational Social Environment

All the previously named motivation techniques focused on methods that you can implement to get motivated; in short: they focused on the motivation from the inside of a person (self-motivation). This motivational technique focuses on a type of motivation that comes from the outside environment of a person: its social environment. The people that surround you (your partner, friends, co-worker and family members) can have an tremendous effect on your motivation. You might have experienced this for yourself if you have ever talked to a really pessimistic person with a lot of negative attitudes. These conversations can be a real pain, as they can cause us to feel similar like them, or we might even adopt similar attitudes. In contrast to this you might feel energized, happy and motivated when you meet some of your best friends and have a good time with them. Surround yourself with energetic and happy people rather than with "complainers" or "demotivators".

PERSONAL DEVELOPMENT MOTIVATION

Personal development motivation is a necessary quality that you need to develop if you want to improve yourself. Most people fail to make any changes in their lives because they lose motivation or don't have it to start with. It does not matter if you want to develop a new skill, change your behaviour or make any other changes. All these goals require a strong motivation behind them.

Ways to get personal development motivation are:

— *Define your personal development goals.* It's very important to know exactly what area of your life you need to improve. If you fail to properly define what you are reaching for you will not achieve much because you will not be motivated by some hazy aims. It's also important that your goals would be appealing to you because the more you want the final outcome, the more motivated you will become to achieve your goals.

— *Review your goals regularly.* It is not enough just to set your goals and never look at them. This will not motivate you because your goals will be out of your sight and out of your mind. To develop personal development motivation you have to constantly look at your goals so that your subconscious mind would start making plans of how to achieve them.

— *Visualize your goals as already achieved.* If you don't believe that you can achieve your goals, you will not. To start believing that you can achieve your desires you should visualize them. When you regularly visualise your goals as already achieved, you will start believing that they can be achieved. This will motivate you and encourage you to take action.

— *Don't give in to the negative inner voice.* If you sometimes get a discouraging negative voice which says that you will not achieve your goals, simply ignore it. Know that it's not the voice of truth, it's just a fear-based voice of your ego. It doesn't mean anything and you should never give up because of a negative self-talk in your head.

How to keep your personal development motivation high

— *Don't lose sight of your goals.* The more often you review your goals, the more personal development motivation you will get. When you keep your goals in front of you, you clearly know where your destination is and every action you take leads you there. Only when you lose sight of your goals you start taking action that leads away from your desires.

- *Take constant action.* To keep the momentum going you absolutely must take action consistently. Taking action will produce results and that will motivate you to keep going. If you stop taking action, your progress will stop. Therefore don't make this mistake and keep going no matter how many obstacles you meet along the way or how many failures you experience.
- *Focus on one goal at a time.* If you find it hard to achieve goals you should focus on one goal at a time. When you progress and achieve a couple of goals this way, you will then be able to set more goals at the same time. If you do that, your personal development motivation will grow because you will see more and more positive results.
- *Remove all the distractions.* To get to your self-improvement goals faster, you should limit the activities that fail to get you closer to your goal (like watching TV or surfing the internet). Also, when you recognise that some activity distracts you from your goals or makes you lose your personal development motivation, you should stop it at once. If you are really serious about progressing in life, you should mainly do things that get you closer to your goals and keep away from the distractions that provide no value in your life.
- *Set priorities.* If you know that there is some hard work that you must do to achieve your goal, don't put it off. You should say to yourself that by

accomplishing it you will tremendously shorten the time of your goal achievement. This will motivate you to complete whatever hard work there is. So you should always do the things that lead to your goals first and do other activities only if you have enough time.

– *Block negative influences.* If someone or something makes you less motivated to achieve your personal development goals, you should eliminate such negative influence at once. Maybe you have friends who don't believe in you or you constantly look at your past and see no real accomplishments. Things as such can easily make you lose your motivation so you cannot afford to focus on them. You should understand that the more you concentrate on things that demotivate you, the quicker you will lose your motivation. So if you have friends who don't believe in you, don't be with them. If you have not achieved anything significant before, stop looking at your past.

Only you know what you are capable of, don't let anyone get you down. Completely ignore everyone that has something negative to say about your goals and desires. You can only achieve something significant when you quit looking at negative things and keep your whole focus on your goals. Goals motivate you and encourage you to keep going whereas negative environment and negative friends discourage you.

WAYS TO IMPROVE YOUR LIFE

How many times have you told yourself that you are going to improve your life, but ended doing nothing? How many times have been dissatisfied with some aspects of your life and vowed to change them, but did not follow through with your decision? What is holding you back, preventing you from improving your life? It is lack of enthusiasm, motivation, desire, determination, willpower and discipline.

Often, especially at the beginning of a new year, people make all kinds of promises to start making changes in their life. This also happens after a reading a book or an article about someone who has attained success or transformed his life. However, the desire to make improvements does not last long, and the enthusiasm quickly wanes away.

So, is it really possible to make positive changes? Yes, it is quite possible, but you have to have a plan, follow certain strategies and act in a certain way.

Improve your life with the following tips:

1. Decide what it is you want to improve. Be specific. Sit down where you can be alone and undisturbed, and make a list of goals. Next, analyze what you have written, to find out whether you really want to achieve the items on your list. You will most probably discover that you don't really want to achieve some of these goals.
2. Write down on another piece of paper the items left in your list, which you really want to achieve. Write them down in the order of their importance for you.
3. Think about a plan, how you can make them come true. Be as practical as possible and use your common sense, intuition, imagination and creativity.
4. Come up with something, even quite minor that you can do right now, such as buying a book with information about your goal, attending a lecture, listening to motivating CDs, looking for courses or workshops that can help you improve your life, or

any other step that will take you closer to achieving your goal.

5. Read inspiring books and articles about people who have attained success in the area of your choice. This will enhance your enthusiasm and motivation.
6. *Visualize* the improvements you want to bring about, as already real and true. Make the mental pictures vivid and alive.
7. Keep your desire, enthusiasm and motivation alive, by thinking often of how you would like your life to look like. Also, think often about the benefits and advantages you will gain by improving your life.
8. Repeat *affirmations*. They will constantly remind you of your goals and programme your subconscious mind to assist you in achieving your aims.
9. Don't let anything deter you from improving your life. Don't give in if there are obstacles, delays or difficulties. Be determined to do what you have decided to do, no matter how much time or effort it takes. This is the way successful people act.
10. Developing strong *willpower and self-discipline* will endow you with the power to overcome any obstacle and difficulty and make you persistent in your efforts. These two skills can be developed through special techniques and exercises.
11. Have faith in yourself and in your ability to improve your life, you financial condition, your habits and your behaviour.
12. Be willing and open to accept change. Don't just say that you want to improve your life. This is not enough. Take action, grab opportunities, and be willing to change your habits and lifestyle.

Remember, making resolutions is not enough; you need to do something about them. If you made resolutions in the past, but did not follow them through, it was because you were not serious enough and your desire was not strong enough.

You can improve your life on all levels, but you need to follow a plan, keep up your enthusiasm, desire and motivation, and don't give in when confronting difficulties and obstacles. It might take some time and effort to improve your life, but this is worthwhile and rewarding goal.

8

LAW OF ATTRACTION

The Law of Attraction is not a new idea. It has always been here from ancient times, and people have always used it. Hunters, who painted scenes of hunting on the walls of caves thousands of years ago, used the law of attraction, as well as modern businessmen, who visualize what they wish to accomplish. You use it too, whenever you think, make plans or daydream.

Books on this subject started to be popular more than a hundred years ago, but the authors of these books did not use the term "the law of attraction". They called it the law of opulence, mental power, mental magic, the power of thoughts or creative visualization. It is the same law, the same power, only with a different name.

In order to take full advantage of the law of attraction you need to know certain rules and follow them. It is true, some people achieve great success, without knowing much or anything about it, but they intuitively use it correctly.

The law of attraction is not a method for getting rich quickly, without doing anything. It requires mental work, focus and visualization, and also the willingness to follow the mental work with any required actions on the physical plane. This law can manifest your desires in many ways, sometimes obviously and directly, and sometimes in an indirect way, through various steps. Sometimes you might attain your goal in a sudden or miraculous way, and at other times slowly or indirectly, one thing leading to another. People might help you, a new job might come along, an idea might pop up in your mind, or your intuition might tell you to follow a certain course of action. These are just a few of the many ways, through which this law can help you manifest your desires.

LAW OF ATTRACTION—MEANING AND DEFINITIONS

The law of attraction is the attractive, magnetic power of the Universe that draws similar energies together. It manifests through the power of creation, everywhere and in multiple ways. Even the law of gravity is part of the law of attraction. This law attracts thoughts, ideas, people, situations and circumstances.

The law of attraction manifests through your thoughts, by drawing to you thoughts and ideas of a similar kind, people who think like you, and also corresponding situations and circumstances. It is the law and power that brings together people of similar interests, who unite into various groups, such as political groups, sports teams, sports fans, fraternities, etc.

You can you take advantage of this law through creative visualization and affirmations. By visualizing a mental image of what you want to achieve or by repeating positive statements, which are called affirmations, you create and bring into your life what you visualize or repeat in your mind. In other words, you use the power of your mind, thoughts, imagination and words.

There have always been people, from ancient times till now, who knew about this law and how to use it. They knew that repeating the same thought day after day, with interest and feeling, causes it to materialize and manifest in their lives.

Here are a few definitions and clarifications about the law of attraction and how it manifests:

- This law is a manifestation of the creative power of the Universe.
- It is through this law that everything is created: galaxies, planets, metals, rocks and even plants, animals and people.
- Like attracts like.
- Thoughts attract corresponding situations and circumstances.
- You get what you think about.
- You attract into your life whatever you focus on.
- Positive thoughts attract positive events. Negative thoughts attract negative events.
- If you entertain feelings and thoughts about hardships and obstacles, then this is what you get.
- If you keep thinking and expecting success, and don't allow doubts enter your mind, you will eventually achieve success.
- It is not enough just to wish for something, you need strong desire and faith to manifest what you want.
- In order for your thoughts to manifest, you have to repeat them often, and add feelings, desire and interest.
- The mind acts like a magnet.
- Similar energy attracts similar energy.
- Your thoughts determine the way you live.
- This law is used by everyone, though mostly unconsciously.

- Filling the mind with worries and anxieties bring stress and unhappiness.
- Filling the mind with happy thoughts will attract happiness into your life.

The Law of Attraction simply says that you attract into your life whatever you think about. Your dominant thoughts will find a way to manifest. But the Law of Attraction gives rise to some tough questions that don't seem to have good answers. However, these problems aren't caused by the Law of Attraction itself but rather by the Law of Attraction as applied to objective reality.

LAW OF ATTRACTION: THE UNIVERSAL LAW

Universal Law of Attraction is as active as the law of Gravity. You just have to become aware and learn a few basic rules about it.

The Law of Attraction has been expressed in various manners. It is beyond doubt that the law of attraction has been active all through. You must have definitely come across following alternate ways of expressing this law:

1. As you sow, so shall you reap.
2. What you put is what you receive?
3. Like attracts like.
4. Law of supply and demand.
5. What comes around goes around?
6. Bible- " As a man think in his hear, so is he."
7. Law of compensation

"What you transmit around in the form of your thoughts, feelings, mental pictures and words, is what you attract into your life". This is how e Ponder, author of Dynamic Law of Prosperity defined the Law of Attraction.

It is a fact that like attracts like. So how is the relevant to you?. When you are focused on what you want you will definitely attract it. On the other side, if you are focused on what you don't want, you attract it too! Each one of us has characteristic of magnet. We attract what we focus on irrespective of whether we need it or not. Also like a magnifying glass, what we focus on gets larger and comes even more quickly into our life.

You must have experienced a situation where you were very focused on accomplishing something. It was the time you were passionate and you were channelising every bit of your energy into achieving it. No force could deter you from accomplishing it. You believed that you deserved and never had a doubt if it was for you. You planned it out and came out with a thumping victory.

Many of us also go through a time when we need something pretty badly, but do not get it. For instance, take money. You wish to have a steady flow of income, but you are not able to. What you think at this time is not about how to create it but other issues like paying bills, money being evil or you just feel that you cant get a steady source of income. The focal point at this point of time should be how to create money, but you do exactly opposite—focus on lack of money. Obviously, this will not help you create it.

So as per the law of attraction, if you focus on negative aspects, things which you don't have, you will only create more scarcity of the same. If you instead shift your focus to what you have, you will increase it. Many a times we say no to many things, wish a lot of things to not happen to us, this makes you focus on the thing and it gets attracted. This is the unique characteristic of Law of Attraction. Whether you wishing for it or not wishing for it is not the issue there. The subject matter of what you wanting or not wanting transmits in the form of waves and ultimately ends up in our life. So be careful when you refuse or do not wish anything.

The good thing to do is to focus on good things and what you want. You should realize that what you want radiate and transmit in the form of mental waves is what you end up attracting into your life. There is nothing more crucial than feeling good. How you feel and where you focus on, is what you will surely attract. This is a fact and you have to accept it.

The universe is abundant. There is no dearth, its only our view of it. There is always ample amount of what you ask and you should strive for it. It is everybody's right to be wealthy and enjoy equally at all levels. There is nothing that you cannot be in this world. You have to build this kind of confidence and mindset into yourself.

Now is the time to use the Law of Attraction to create things that we need. You can have all that you desire in life. You have to build the confidence in yourself that you can achieve anything in life. Be very cautious as to what you think and feel. Thoughts and feelings which make you feel good will help you in a great way in attracting what you want in your life.

The Law of Attraction brings you *what you think about*. To think is to ask. Every thought is an intention. The Law of Attraction is totally neutral—it doesn't filter what you ask for. If you think about what you want, you get it. If you think about what you don't want, you get that too.

If you want to manifest your desires, then it makes no sense to write statements like the above. Even when your desires haven't yet manifested, remain hopeful and optimistic. Pour on the positive intent, and allow the Law of Attraction to work with you. Stay in the present moment. Be on the lookout for synchronicities. If you start getting frustrated, take a walk or do a meditation to nip it in the bud. Otherwise you'll negate your desires by intending their opposite.

The key to mastering the Law of Attraction is responsibility. You must accept personal responsibility for everything in your life. If you perceive it, you've manifested it. Whatever you give your attention to will expand.

DISCOVER THE POWER OF THE LAW OF ATTRACTION

The law of attraction is an immensely powerful law which can drive drastic changes in everybody's life. The law of attraction has been active all through in your life. What you have to do now is become aware of it and learn how to leverage it for you won benefit. The three things the law of attraction does for you are:

1. *Draws things similar to who you are.* Note that above I said "who" you are and not "what you want". There is a huge difference between the two. What you want may not mean you will achieve it. To gain it you have to adapt an attitude which will attract it to your life. As you initiate and implement these change you will notice that the law of attraction does work.
2. *Gives your life a direction:* The law of attraction plays an important role to direct your life. Whatever comes into your life directly or indirectly affects your life. Hence it is very important to have positive things happening in your life. If you are unsatisfied with your current life, chances are that you have been heading in the wrong direction. This direction was a direct result of the things you have done in the past.
3. *Transform your life for good.* The most crucial things for you to grasp is that whatever has happened to you in life—good or bad is because you attracted them into your life. So if you want to attract certain things you have to change your ways and personality. Once you bring about these changes

your life will get transformed in a way you might not have imagined earlier.

Each individual has a lot of untapped potential in himself. Are you aware that every experience that you have undergone in life till now is because of your thoughts and emotions behind these thoughts? Examine your life. You are happy with some of the conditions and unhappy with some. Most of us end up believing that we are a victim of destiny. But that is far away from truth. Life is a beautiful game and like every game it also has Laws which we need to understand in depth to win this game.

The Law of Attraction, is undoubtedly the strongest of all the Universal Laws. To put it in few words "Like attracts like" or "That which is likened unto itself is drawn". It means that whatever we focus on by means of our thoughts, we will have it in our life. If we focus on what we want we will attract it, on the other hand, if we focus on what we don't want we will attract it too!

The Law is very simple. Our thoughts are very haphazard and short living. For instance, when you say " I want a brand new trendy sportscar", the same moment the Universe begins deliberations for your wish to become a reality. But then in the same breath you say "But I can't afford it" and you dispel all that Universe was deliberating to make your wish come true.

Now that you are aware about the mechanism of the Law, make use of it. When you wish for something, say, a sportscar, but feel you can't afford it become aware that you are transmitting thoughts which convey the message of scarcity. So you end up with being more scarce. So by changing our thoughts and emotions we can use them like a magnet to attract what we want?

To give another instance, let us consider money. You have been wanting money for a long time now. Just examine what you feel each time you think about money. Do you feel happy, elated or do you end up angry and disappointed? You may be even envious of those of have it. Most people are always emotionally confused when it comes to money. You need not worry. No matter how sad or frustrated you have felt, you can still change it. Just consciously practice the Law of Attraction by altering your thoughts and feelings and you will have money flowing into your life soon.

The Law of Attraction is a guiding beacon for everyone who wants to change conditions of his/her life. You just need to understand how this law works and use it to your benefit. Initiate activities to alter your thoughts and you can change a lot of things. What you should be aware is the kind of emotions and feelings you garner on a particular subject. That is a true measure of how you feel. Another scale to measure is the conditions of your life. Your emotions will be of the greatest assistance to you when you want to judge the energy and waves that you are transmitting. Emotions never lie.

PROCESS OF DELIBERATE ATTRACTION

Below are some simple steps that will help you clarify what your real "wants" are. Further, it will help you in dealing with any doubts you have and help you overcome the Inner Critic.

1. Know what you want.
2. Visualize your wish
3. Be Alert

Know what you Want. Be aware of what you want. Practice this. Take any topic like, discovering the ideal partner, creation of wealth, being a great author, buying your ideal house etc. This is my personal belief that the law of attraction will always work best when you want something that is helpful to others.

Visualize your wish as fulfilled. Know what you want. To do this, you can list all things you wish. At times, you will know what you don't want. Use this to know what you want. For example, if you know that you don't want your house to be an hour away from office, you can use it to state that you want your house to be 10 minutes away from office. Make it sure that all you wish is stated in a positive manner. The next step is to visualize your wish as fulfilled. Just imagine what you would do or what the circumstance would be when your wish is fulfilled. If possible, imagine every tiny detail of such a situation.

Be Alert: Many a times, our Inner Critic makes us doubt our capability. When this happens, cut it at the root. Change your attitude. Do anything or activity that will break all your inhibitions. Go for a walk, a drive or divert yourself into activity in which you will get involved. This will make you ignore the Inner Critic. Another method is to just tell the voice to be silent.

To quell all self-doubts appreciate all that you can find around you. Notice anything and everything, big or small and appreciate it.

Be alert to opportunities that the universe provides us. Nature will provide you all the ingredients and opportunities to grab and make the most. You have to be alert to recognize such an opportunity and use it for your benefit.

TIPS FOR BEING PROSPEROUS

A prosperous life doesn't mean having a lot of money only. If you want to be truly prosperous, you have to transform your mind set in a major way. You have to think about abundance rather than thinking about lack of it. You have to shift a lot of levels higher in all spheres of your life.

The following 10 tips will help you do that:

1. *Indulge in Your Passion*: When you indulge in things that you are passionate about, you will feel happy and satisfied. When you feel happy, you emit positive vibrations and hence attract things that are of the same frequency as yours. Hence start investing time in things that you really love doing. It could be a hobby now, try to make a living out of it.
2. *Affirm You Always Have More Than Enough* The more you pay attention to lack of things in your life, the more you will attract it. You can stop this by telling yourself that you have enough of what you need. The more you believe in this, the more you will see the change in the environment surrounding you.
3. *Act*: Though you need not work towards attaining abundance, but doing so wont harm you in any manner. Rather it will be quicken your want for abundance. So don't just sit around expecting circumstances to change—take control and change them yourself! One small step in the direction you wish may open many opportunities onto you. It could boost your self-esteem and give you a sense of control in your life.
4. *Be Thankful and Appreciative*: If you are appreciative you will always look at the positive aspect of anything. You will feel more abundant and be thankful for the same. Hence never forget to appreciate and be thankful for whatever life has given you. Even small things need to be appreciated. The more you practice this, the more you will attract better things in your life. It will do wonders in your life.

5. *Love*: One of the most powerful and transformational forces is love. It can be a great healer if you are in pain, can bring you abundance and motive you to do things which you have never done earlier. Hence love all those who come into your life. Love your family, friends and even people who are difficult to handle and talk to. Love all your troubles and difficulties. Love will give you the strength to combat any adverse situation.
6. *Improve your Self-Image*: What you believe in will influence a lot on what you experience in your day to day life. If you don't feel the abundance, you will never be able to attract it. Hence start boosting the image you have about yourself and constantly remind yourself that you deserve all the happiness in this world. Accept every gift with gratitude. The more gratitude you show, the more you will be able to open yourself up to receive whatever the universe has to give you.
7. *Create Space*: If you jam up your life with negative things, there will be no room to store whatever good comes up in your life. Hence, make room for good things to come. Shed the negative inhibitions you have nurtured till now. Shun those painful emotional feelings and forget the issues you have. Purify yourself physically, mentally, emotionally and spiritually. This way you will be open up and create a lot of space for good things to be stored in your life.
8. *Change Your Beliefs:* Apart from poor self-esteem, you may be nourishing other kind of negative belief which limit you even further from receiving any prosperity. This could be your belief that you have to toil hard to get money or that rich people are haughty and unhelpful or you may feel that a lot of wealth is a burden. Hence examine each of

your beliefs and eliminate the one which limit you. This is a process you should never stop doing. Examine your beliefs at every point in life.

9. *Observe The Abundance You Have Around You*: Whatever you focus on grows. This is true even for prosperity. Hence always seek abundance wherever you go. While you shop, notice the abundance of the merchandise around you. Each of such product was someone's idea, which has now become so abundant. Go to the vegetable market and observe the abundance there. Each vegetable was nothing but a seed planted which grew to its present form. Find out time to observe the abundance you have around you and you will definitely attract more of it.
10. *Be Positive*: If you are positive, the thoughts you have are positive and emotions you will are positive, then for sure you will attract positive conditions into your life. If you want to be prosperous, this is a way that will work for sure. Negative thinking is a tendency to focus on the negative aspects of life. But even that is an opportunity in disguise. The more you condition your mind to look for opportunities, the more positive you will become, thereby attracting more of positive things into your life. Hence start becoming positive right now. This will surely bring a drastic change in things you experience on a daily basis.

Law of Attraction can truly bring a dramatic change in your life. To do this you should know the mechanism and use it to your advantage. You certainly must be knowing a lot of people who seem to have great things in their lives. Ever wondered why it happens to them. Don't worry its not very tough to figure it out.

LAW OF ATTRACTION AND YOUR BELIEFS

A very common misconception among people about the law of attraction is about their beliefs. Not many realize how strong and crucial beliefs can be for an individual. By belief I don't mean believing in the law of attraction. I mean the belief that you have had and which made you what you are today. Beliefs definitely play a vital role in what kind of success you will achieve.

If you want to be successful, but you don't feel you are worthy of it, your actions will clearly give an indication. If you do not act like people who have been successful you will never walk the path of success. What you believe in influence your actions and the things that you attract into your life depend on your actions.

The beliefs that you have inculcated in your mind till now play a very important role in what you attract into your life. Surprised on hearing this? I am sure you must have come across people who ponder why some things happen to them only. If you analyze a bit you will realize that their beliefs made those things happen. So examine your own beliefs. Who knows, they might be the reason you not achieving things you wish.

To put it more clearly, I will give you an example. Every actions we do is as a result of our attitude. And every action has a result. Thus our attitude makes us act in a particular fashion and hence is responsible for the results too. Let me give you an instance: Assume that you are at a party where the participants include both humans and Martians. Now we are all conditioned to believe that Martians are thieves, cheaters and not at all trustworthy. Now, suppose after about half an hour at the party you find that you have lost your wrist watch. How would you react? You will obviously suspect the Martians of stealing your watch. And now you interrogate each and every Martian about your watch.

You bad mouth them and end up fighting with them. In the meanwhile, one of your pals finds the watch and after finding you hands it over to you. He tells that you had forgotten it on the kitchen table.

Thus, your belief that Martians are thieves attracted a fight. Beliefs shape up your attitude and govern the pattern of your behaviour. So do examine the beliefs that you currently have and find out if there are any that are hindering things that you want from coming to you.

LAW OF ATTRACTION AND EXCEPTIONS

The law of attraction is being talked about a lot lately and chances are that you have implemented some of the rules you learnt. But you may not be satisfied with the results. You may even be thinking if the law is true or just a fictitious concept. Is the law of attraction applicable to you?

Believe me, the law of attraction has been active in your life for a very long period of time. Most happenings in your life are because you attracted them. This may sound incredible to you but it is a fact you will have to accept sooner or later. The law of attraction is working for you though you may feel otherwise.

The matter that you should focus on is how to begin attracting what you want. Every one on this earth is subject to the law of attraction. There are no exceptions. The only reason why things have not happened to you is that have not taken the appropriate steps. Like every field has laws which are always applicable the law of attraction also follows rules no matter what. So think about things that you need to plan and do differently. You are attracting something in your life, so now is the right moment to start attracting what you wish. You may require some time figuring out what needs to be done, but it is only you who will have to implement these changes. So do not waste time wondering if the law of attraction is applicable to you. Instead, examine things that you do for their appropriateness in attracting things that you wish.

HOW CAN BENEFIT FROM THE LAW OF ATTRACTION?

Each of us is a live magnet. The people, circumstances that come into our lives are always very similar to the thoughts that are very prominent in our minds.

All the success in our life, be it in the professional or personal arena is governed by this law. The law of attraction is know to human beings since a long time. Egyptian mystery schools wrote about it around 3000 years before Christ. Every thing that you do, speak is because of this law. It is omnipresent.

The Law of Attraction has been expressed in a number of ways by many people. Some very common forms are "Like attracts like", "Birds of a feather flock together" and many more.

Never underestimate the power of your thoughts. They are a kind of mental energy that propagates as fast as light. No barrier is too tough for them. Many times it must have happened that you are thinking about a person and the next instant the person is calling you. You are not aware but your thoughts were connected to the person about whom you were thinking.

Everything that has happened to you till now in your life is due the kind of person you are. Changing how you think will also change the things that you attract. The only thing that you have to do is change yourself and you will turn a new leaf in your life.

Every field in governed by some fundamental laws and they work no matter what. The law of attraction is no exception. The more practical issue that one should think about is how to make the law of attraction work so that you benefit in the same way as others have.

The truth is the law of attraction has been always bearing fruits for you. If you happen to be living a mediocre lifestyle it is because all activities you have done till now have been so. A person who has done things above average is leading an above average life! Hence the law of attraction was always there. It was you who failed to notice it.

Examine the life of people who have had success in life. Notice all activities they started doing differently, rather than following their earlier methods. You will definitely discover that they started doing things in a fashion that attracted what they wanted. For example, they could taste success in business because they proactively took measures to carry out activities that would make them successful.

9

CREATIVE VISUALIZATION

"Creative Visualization" is a wonderful phrase to capture a concept that is foundational to all manifestations in life. "Dreaming" and "Visioning" and "Imagery" and "Mental Imagery" and "Imagination" and "Expectation" convey similar ideas. More important than choosing the perfect word or phrase is to understand the ideas.

We are always individually developing ourselves and creating our own individual lives. We create with a combination of these: (*1*) desires and dreams, (2) thoughts and images, (*3*) language in writing or speaking, and (*4*) actions. In our culture, many people believe that actions, and only actions, get results. It's the combination of these, in alignment with each other that create the *desired* results.

The concept of "creative visualization" combines aspects of (*1*) and (2) in the list above. All life grows because of desires and the thoughts associated with the desires. All through the day, you have a variety of desires: to breathe, to interact with others, to open the door, to eat, to sleep, to walk to your car, to do a good job, to relax, etc. How you think about each reflects and determines your relationship to it.

Intentional creative imagery can be focused on any subject, and on any aspect of any subject. Keep in mind, you're creating negative experiences if your images include primarily negative thoughts; you're creating positive experiences if your creative dreaming includes primarily positive thoughts. It's quite common to have a combination of positive and negative thoughts, so you may find yourself experiencing a combination of positive and negative situations.

DREAM THE DREAM YOU WANT TO LIVE

In order to create the situation you want to live, you must think the thoughts, dream the dreams, and speak the words that are in resonance with your desires. You can do this in the day-to-day, moment-to-moment situations in your life. You can do it for the long-term dreams or goals, also, but when you start practicing in the immediate situation right in front of you right now, it becomes so much easier to apply the approach to longer term dreams and desires. You experience what you think about, what you dream about.

Creative visualization is powerful. It is the basis for your tomorrow. For me, creative visualizing and breathing are in the same category of importance: both are essential for a satisfying life. Surely, not everyone uses creative imagination or visualization in the same way or to the same level of benefit, but it is an act of creation. Not everyone uses creative visualization intentionally; in fact, it's rather commonplace to be careless about thoughts, imaginations, and dreaming. These are not as private as most people think they are.

So, you be as intentional and positive as you can about your creative imaginings. When you expect a presentation to your boss will be poorly received, you're using negative creative imagery. For better results, change your expectations and images so that you pave the way for a well-prepared, well-received presentation.

When you imagine being embarrassed on the tennis court or golf course, stimulate some creative visualization about a winning game of tennis or golf. When you're considering a variety of approaches to ease a relationship, use positive mental images creatively.

Creative visualization is a power that is your birthright—it comes with the human package. How you use it is your choice. When you use it with high intention, integrity, and joy, you are empowered!

POWER OF CREATIVE VISUALIZATION

Creative visualization is a mental technique that uses the imagination to make dreams come true. Used in the right way, creative visualization can improve our life and attract success and prosperity. It is a power that can alter our environment and circumstances, cause events to happen, and attract money, possessions, work, people and love into our life. Creative visualization uses the power of the mind, and is the power behind every success.

By visualizing a certain event or a situation, or an object, such as a car, a house, furniture etc., we attract it into our life. It is a process that is similar to daydreaming. For some people, this might look like magic, but there is no magic involved, only the natural process of the power of thoughts and natural mental laws. It is like having a genie at your disposal!

There are people who use this technique naturally in their everyday affairs, not being aware that they are using some sort of power. All successful people use it consciously or unconsciously, attracting the success they want into their life, by visualizing their goals as already accomplished.

Thoughts are endowed with a creative power that molds our life, and attracts what we think about.

Thoughts travel from one mind to another, and if they are strong enough, they can be unconsciously picked up by people, who are in a position to help us achieve our desires and goals.

We are part of the Omnipotent Power that has created the universe, and therefore, we participate in the process of creation. Bearing this thought in mind, there is no wonder that thoughts materialize. Stop for a moment and think—You are an indivisible part of the great Universal Power! This means that your thoughts can come true! Not all thoughts of course, but those that are concentrated, well-defined, and often-repeated often.

Thought is energy, especially a concentrated thought laden with emotional energy. Thoughts change the balance of energy around us, and bring changes to the environment in accordance with them.

There is another explanation why visualization brings results. It may come as a surprise to most, but the theory of "Maya"—Illusion, which comes from the eastern philosophies, provides the explanation.

According to the Indian philosophy "Advaita-Vedanta", which is called "Nonduality" in the West, the world is not real, but only an illusion, created by our thoughts. Since most people think and repeat the same or similar thoughts often, focusing their mind and thoughts on their current environment, they create and recreate the same sort of events or circumstances. This process preserves the same "world" and status quo. It is like watching the same film over and over again, but we can change the film by changing our thoughts and visualize different circumstances and life, and in this way create a different "reality". For us, it is a reality, though in fact it is just a dream we call "reality".

By changing our thoughts and mental images, we change our "Reality"; we change the "illusory" world we believe we live in. We are not employing magic or supernatural powers when creating and changing our life and circumstances. It is not something "Material" that we change; we only change our thoughts, which shape our world.

All this is like dreaming a very realistic dream, and then changing the dream. We are not awakening from the dream, just changing the dream. So why not change your dreams to something more satisfying? If you live in small apartment and need a larger one, instead of brooding about your fate and lack of money, change your thoughts and visualize and believe that you are living in a bigger apartment.

Overcoming Limited Thinking

Creative visualization can do great things, but for every person, there are some areas, which he or she might find hard to change, at least in the immediate future. The power of visualization is a mighty power, but there are some limits to using it. These limits are within us, not in the power.

We often limit ourselves and cannot look beyond a limited circle. We limit ourselves by our thoughts and beliefs. The more open-minded we can be, and the bigger we dare to think, the greater are our opportunities and possibilities. Limitations are within our minds, and it is up to us to rise above them. It may take some time until things start to change. Simple, small demonstrations of this power may come fast, but bigger results may need a longer time to happen. The time and effort put forth in this study are really worthwhile. Have faith and patience and results will start appearing.

Making Creative Visualization Work

Some guidelines for effective creative visualization are given below:

- Define your goal.
- Think, meditate and listen to your intuition to ascertain that you really desire to attain this goal.
- Ascertain that only good will result from your visualization, for you and for others.
- Sit alone in a quiet place, where you will not be disturbed.
- Relax your body.
- Breathe rhythmically and deeply several times.
- Visualize a clear and detailed mental image of what you desire to get or accomplish.
- Use in your imagination all the five senses of sight, hearing, touch, smell and taste.
- Add desire and feelings into what your mental image.
- Visualize at least twice a day, about 10 minutes each time.
- Persevere with your visualization, day after day, with, patience, hope and faith.
- Stay positive, thinking positive thoughts, feeling positive feelings and using positive words.
- During the day, when negative thoughts and doubts arise, replace them with positive thoughts. As each negative thought enters your mind, immediately substitute it with a positive thought.
- Keep an open mind, so that you recognize opportunities and take advantage of them.
- After concluding your visualization session, say attentively and earnestly, "Let everything happen in a harmonious and favorable way for all involved".

Use the power of imagination only for your and others' good, and never try to use it to get something that belongs to others or hurt others. Make sure that what you are creating is good for all involved, and cause no harm to your environment.

Though the manifestation of your goal might sometimes happen in a sudden and expected manner, most of the time it will happen in a natural and gradual manner, one thing leading to another. If you desire money, it won't necessarily drop on your head from the sky or you will win it in the lottery. It will more probably come through a new job, promotion, a business deal or through various other channels.

Our thoughts and feelings, and the mental images we carry in our mind, affect our life. By changing them we change our life. This means that we have to be careful with our thoughts and how we feel about them, otherwise we might get things and enter into situations that you do not want, and then we will have to find ways to get rid of them. Better think and visualize what that we really and truly want, and which will improve our life.

CREATIVE VISUALIZATION—A KEY TO SUCCESS

You can harness the power of creative visualization to help you improve every area of your life. It is a power you use everyday, whether you are conscious of it or not. With the knowledge of the laws and rules governing creative visualization, and a conscious and effective use of them, you can fill your life with success.

Health, success, money, promotion and possessions can be gained through creative visualization. It does not mean that everything will change overnight. Mental work is necessary. A change of attitude towards life is a necessity. You need an open mind, concentration, the ability to visualize, and a lot of enthusiasm and persistence. Suppose you need five thousand dollars. Build in your imagination a mental image of a check for this amount, made out in your name. See it clearly as if it is really there, but do not visualize the name of the bank, or who signed it.

Imagine yourself holding the check. Pass your fingers over it to feel its texture. A clear cut mental image, involving all the five senses, and soaked with desire and faith is a power that influences your actions and imprints itself on the creative power of the universe.

Arouse in yourself feelings of happiness and satisfaction that you have received this check. Do not think who gave it to you, or why it was drawn in your name.

Imagining that you have already received the check is very important. This way the subconscious mind accepts it as a fact and does not arouse hindrances. It is also important to feel convinced that it came in a harmonious way, and that all people involved were and are benefited by it.

The next step is to see yourself depositing the check in your account at the bank. You may also visualize the entry for five thousand dollars in your bank's statement.

What will happen? The money will appear in your life. It may come through various channels. It may come as a present, winning at the lottery, a promotion at work, a new job, a good investment in shares or stocks, or through other channels. Results may be immediate or delayed.

Day-dreams are the first stage, but day -dreams alone are not sufficient. Do not make the mistake of mixing up creative visualization and daydreaming. They are two different things. The former may give some pleasure, but employing the latter correctly is utilizing a real power.

What you visualize can materialize through various ways and channels. Sometimes it may manifest in a fast, sudden and unusual manner, but mostly it manifests in a most natural and gradual manner, one thing leading to another.

Creative visualization, which is conscious desire and visualization of a goal, can change your life and take you out of the circle of mere chance and luck. Visualizing the successful outcome of an event, and focusing your mental energy on it, tend to draw it to you. It is not hocus-pocus. Creative visualization is the key to success. It is a natural mighty natural power. Everyone possesses this power in some degree and even uses it, but in unconscious and negative way.

Most people have no control over their thoughts, and tend to think negatively most of the time, and therefore they bring negative results into their lives. It is when one becomes conscious of this mighty power, studies it and learns how to use it effectively, that positive results start to arrive. Using creative visualization consciously, and in the correct manner, is the key to the door of success. There are some important rules and laws to follow in order to achieve success. Certain traits of character and skills are necessary too, such as faith in yourself and in your abilities, patience, perseverance, concentration, willpower, self-discipline and strong ambition.

Creative Visualization and Daily Tasks

Creative visualization can help us in our daily tasks, by making everything flow more easily, and with less energy expenditure. We constantly shape our daily events of life with our creative visualization power. Sometimes we like what we create and sometimes we don't. A little more attention to our thoughts and imagination can make a great difference. This method is useful in almost every daily situation. When for example, you know you going to have difficult day at work, or you have to meet someone you dread, this technique is very handy. You need to visualize the situation, as you would like it to be. You see the other person treating you in a friendly respectful way, and that's what happens.

When a situation is visualized with full attention, it has its effect on the subconscious mind. It causes us to see the world differently, relate to people in a more constructive way, and grant us inner power, energy and faith. This influences our behavior and whomever we meet. Our thoughts are transmitted telepathically to our surroundings, influencing subtly the people we meet.

Creative visualization backed by attention and faith works. You can easily influence your daily life events, by using creative visualization. This technique can help you accomplish everything faster, with less strain and energy expenditure, and keep you feeling happy and satisfied.

Visualizing and Letting Go

If you have read about creative visualization you have most probably been told to visualize, and then release the mental image to the Universe, otherwise it won't materialize. In other words, visualize several times a day for several minutes, and then forget for the rest of the day what you have visualized.

Common sense says that the more you visualize, the faster you get results. It is reasonable to believe that if you keep the mental image of your goal constantly in your mind, it will materialize faster. So why are you told not to think of your goal the rest of the day? It is not that if you hold the image constantly in your mind it cannot manifest in your life. It is not that you have to release it, because if you keep it stuck in your mind it won't materialize. The reason is very simple. Most people do not have control over their minds. Most people have doubts and little faith, when thinking about goals and ambitions. Their minds are inclined to negative thinking and worrying.

It is usually possible to hold the mind on a goal or desire for only a few minutes, before it starts interfering with opposite thoughts. You have most probably seen how after a few minutes of visualization, doubts and impatience rise up, which makes it difficult to concentrate and keep thinking positively. This means that if you keep thinking about your goal for too long, you will unconsciously start to sabotage all your previous positive visualization, and consequently accomplish nothing.

During the day, while engaged in various activities, the predominant mental attitude rules, and if it is negative, any thinking about your goal will be negative too. Only if you are well trained in concentration, and positive thinking became a habit with you, it will be possible for you to think positively about your goals, at any time of the day.

There is another reason why it is advisable to let go. Visualization activates your subconscious mind, which consequently sharpens your intuition, brings you useful ideas concerning your goals, and inspires and motivates you to achieve them.

By releasing the mental image, you free your conscious mind to become aware of the prompting of the subconscious mind. You make it possible for the subconscious mind to bring important information to your conscious mind. This action makes you become more aware of opportunities that pop up, and let the subconscious mind motivate you to take action, instead of just waiting for things to happen.

SELECTED READINGS

Abraham Harold Maslow, Robert, Frager, James Fadimàn, *Motivation and Personality,* HarperCollins Publishers, January 1987.

Arnold M. Washton, *Willpower's Not Enough: Recovering from Addictions of Every Kind,* William Morrow Paperbacks, September 26, 1990.

Bill Johnson, Dick Mills, Randy Clark, Jack Taylor, *The Supernatural Power of a Transformed Mind: Access to a Life of Miracles,* Destiny Image Publishers, January 1, 2005.

Bill Johnson, *The Supernatural Power of a Transformed Mind: Access to a Life of Miracles,* Destiny Image, 1 January 2005.

Gary Null, *Gary Null's Mind Power,* Signet, June 5 2007.

Harry Lorayne, *Secrets of Mind Power,* Pustak Mahal, 16 December 2004.

Ian McMahan, Joseph Murphy, *The Power of Your Subconscious Mind: One of the Most Powerful Self-help Guides Ever Written!* Pocket Books; Revised edition edition, 3 January 2006.

James Borg, *Mind Power: Change Your Thinking, Change Your Life,* Prentice Hall Life, 21 Oct 2010.

James Goi Jr., *How to Attract Money Using Mind Power,* Infinity Publishing, November 7, 2007.

Jim Randel, *The Skinny on Willpower: How to Develop Self Discipline,* Rand Media Co, February 1, 2009.

John Baldoni, *Great Motivation Secrets of Great Leaders,* McGraw-Hill; 1 edition, December 23, 2004.

John Kehoe, *Mind Power into the 21st Century: Techniques to Harness the Astounding Powers of Thought,* Zoetic, April 1, 1997.

John Kehoe, Nancy Fischer, *Mind Power for Children,* Zoetic, October 2002.

Joseph Murphy, *The Power of Your Subconscious Mind,* Wilder Publications, November 24, 2008.

Kelly McGonigal, *The Willpower Instinct: How Self-Control Works, Why It Matters, and What You Can Do To Get More of It*, Avery December 29, 2011.

Lawrence LeShan, *How to Meditate: A Guide to Self-Discovery*, Little, Brown and Company, September 14, 1999.

Michael J. Losier, Law of Attraction: *The Science of Attracting More of What You Want and Less of What You Don't*, Michael J. Losier; 2 edition, October 31, 2004.

Mouni Sadhu, *Concentration: A Guide to Mental Mastery*, Wilshire Book Company; Revised edition, December 1980.

Norman Vincent Peale, *The Power of Positive Thinking*, Ballantine Books, August 27, 1996.

Phillip Cooper, *Secrets of Creative Visualization*, Red Wheel/Weiser; Auflage: illustrated edition, 19 March 1995.

Prabha Rani, *How to Develop Self Confidence and Influence People*, Sublime Publications, 2011.

Rakesh K. Mittal, *Positive Mind Power: Lessons from Real Life*, Sterling, 2005.

Ralph Waldo Trine, *The Higher Powers of Mind and Spirit*, Kindle Edition, Public Domain Books, March 17, 2006.

Rob Yeung, *Personality: How to Unleash Your Hidden Strengths*, Prentice Hall Life, 20 August 2009.

Roy F. Baumeister, John Tierney, *Willpower: Rediscovering the Greatest Human Strength*, Penguin Press HC, September 1, 2011.

Shakti Gawain, *Creative Visualization: Use the Power of Your Imagination to Create What You Want in Your Life*. New World Library, Nataraj; 25th anniversary edition, September 19, 2002.

Steve Chandler, *100 Ways To Motivate Yourself: Change Your Life Forever*, Career Pr Inc; Revised edition, September 2004.

Theron Q. Dumont, *The Power of Concentration*, Kessinger Publishing, LLC, March 5, 2004.

Victor Davich, *8 Minute Meditation: Quiet Your Mind. Change Your Life.*, Perigee Trade, July 6, 2004.

William Walker Atkinson, *Mind Power: The Secret of Mental Magic*, CreateSpace, November 18, 2010.

William Walker Atkinson, *The Law of Attraction: or Thought Vibration in the Thought World*, Wilder Publications, September 23, 2007.